VICTOR LEONARD LIBERMANN

DIVIDED HEROES
THE PRISONERS WITH OPEN DOORS

HUMANS AGAINST MACHINES
Modus Vivendi

novum pro

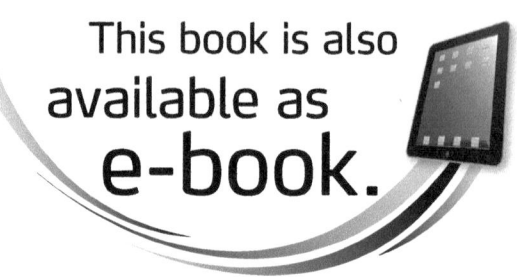

www.novum-publishing.co.uk

All rights of distribution, including via film, radio, and television, photomechanical reproduction, audio storage media, electronic data storage media, and the reprinting of portions of text, are reserved.

Printed in the European Union on environmentally friendly, chlorine- and acid-free paper.

© 2019 novum publishing

ISBN 978-3-99064-562-8
Editing: Julie Hoyle, B.Ed (Hons)
Cover photos: Dmitry Kotin,
Beatrice Preve | Dreamstime.com
Cover design, layout & typesetting:
novum publishing

www.novum-publishing.co.uk

Extracts of subjects in subversive attendance

THE PRISONERS WITH OPEN DOORS

Methodology
Micro-technical to macro-technical
intensive philosophy in augmented process,
for structural adjustments in new social architectures,
capable to overcome any financial or institutional crisis

Sort
Philosophy, Lyrics, Poetry, Politics,
Literature, Sociology, Psychology,
Principles of Progressive Economics
for independent independences

THE MASTER BOOK

Introductory

*Philosophy
in the poetry
of a song*

Introduction

Philosophy is now, yesterday and an hour before eternity
as every day's press conference of wisdom,
in everyone's thoughts, but almost no one's actions
fact absorbed in adumbrated consciousnesses of a shaded time
which transmutes us all into prisoners with open doors
an unfortified muted consensus divides our societies
when we can choose never to die, if we dare to,
the centuries inside us oppress for the momentum
haunted in a journey of seductions among
the perishable and the imperishable

Sincerely yours,
Victor Leonard Libermann

General Manager: Matthijs Volkers
Creative Manager: Anastasios Simeonidis
Product Manager: Alexander Eric Geist
Author: Victor Leonard Libermann

Intellectual property/Copyrights 2018

Simplified Short Biography

I was born in a foreigners' land, unchallenged its drought from ideas, inappropriate ever to be my home. I started to search in a period which was changing skin and real revolutions didn't want to be confirmed. This fundamental unknown forced me to walk on rough pathways, to be the impossible, my only friend, to make me able to drive on the new highways of understanding, to finally find the country of my heart, where I always belong, to be a stranger no more; with premature name, preserved in values from time, to be bequeathed a profound civilization, flawlessly willingly to retreat from the weaknesses of strength and a new currency, which still needs muscles to build foundations, where everybody is me, is you, is us. I wired Nations of Babel, different on papers, but homogeneous souls, sculpted in the depth of distance, destined the one to be the fulfillment of the other, totally capable to create a vision for a greater world.

Through the courtesy of reliable true expectations, I received the heavy duty to honor as I was honored and I gave everything I got, without reckoning the balances of enough, to meet the limits of the limitless,one day anyone's honest, creative or selfless efforts to count, as faithful adjustments of a global impact;the tear of any pain to heal, by waiting the one of happiness, unnecessary its duration to be considered,the availability of forward fearless to wake and sleep with the same exacting dream, till it becomes reality.

CEO of International Projects
Victor Leonard Libermann
Waking and sleeping with the same vision, till it becomes reality and then the past will start demolishing the intensity to teach serenity to be bright to make it competent to build our future

Foundations

Only the capacity to risk everything from the start for the deepest beliefs,
sourced from moral inspirations, can achieve the impossible.
Initiatives are building, brick by brick, the walls of evolution.
We are born in a war of unfairness, any obstacle or boundary
shouldn't diminish our visibility for true justice.
Actions must be an honor
for the strong commitments of real living.

Sample:
part of 'Faith of Attraction'

The numbers
attract the body
the beauty
attracts the heart
the faith
attracts the mind
to find the way for the soul
to become spirit

The Compass

Debt crisis approves the system's failure and must be renewed to reproduce a sustainable future for us and the coming generations. People are running the system without knowing it and for every problem, they see responsibility somewhere else. The mentality of each one of us empowers or heals painful mistakes. Truth can be understood only if we watch it as cold-blooded spectators and not through personal interests; any less a criteria pushes the probability of reparation further. When time passes with ignorance, solutions vanish. The easy will become unapproachable and common sense invisible. As an effect, common interest will be no longer reachable and the decay of the few will become the mass spiritual nutrition. The availability of the obvious has its limits to contribute.

In a virtual world corruption is stronger than creation, with invalid securities and the pioneers' pipeline from knowledge to wisdom disoriented. Crisis brings the urgency for reality and boosts the maturity for evolution. It depends if societies choose to defend their weaknesses or gain constructive character capable of expanding their fulfillment. Automatic mechanisms to obtain sustainable growth can't be invented, because improvement needs continuous progress. Every step shows new horizons with the wide-open spectrum on top. Consciousness must be immediately alerted when the lack of creation appears or sooner, when rare spices we use become luxury. The unsupported brightness is the main witness for the uninvited privilege for justice. The force to foresee is within all.

Our artificial intelligence can learn from the easy or the difficult way of life, can be wise through responsibility or greedy through vanity. Wealth not based on perpetual values just consumes energy inside a dead end. The acceptance of an unrealistic power without stable foundations doesn't seek virtues any longer, but addictions, blindfolded from the arrogance of nothing. Creation is the only noble certificate proving ethics and courte-

sy. The uniqueness of our existence can't be endured with dictations of the past or the fear of an unknown tomorrow.

The fields of civilization need the seed of self-awareness destined to grow from an unchallenged light, prepared to generate visions for self-realization. The few successful gain the duty to enrich the environment for more, because it is everyone's mission. Generations hand in hand must transmit the intellectuality for new milestones. Silent drops of any kind of talents can assemble for a fair ocean. Ingratitude eliminates the gravity for precious beliefs.

The illusion of multilevel interests is just provoking necessary changes and abusing perspectives. Only priceless obdurate oaths sourced from truthful judgment, echo within all divergent views, ordains prosperity. The reasons are manufacturing pulses to reconstruct the tower of Babel, from the vastness of the possible. The word can be initiated.

HUMANS AGAINST MACHINES
(Inclusive)

Intellectual Coherence

Characteristics & Morphology

This subversive laconic compact content can be also characterized as modern economic philosophy, without any discrimination of gender, race or status, to motivate any individual to meet successfully higher aims; altogether to avoid and reduce debts by diminishing the rates of unemployment with structural employment, where machines can't replace humans. A strong impulse from the micro-technical to macro-technical philosophy, which brings an entity in to the world; to support even a drop which thought to become a lake.

  This compressed philosophy is structured as lyrics, to be read more easily. Its accessibility is shaped with the main bodies, the steps, to be addressed the refrains which express the central messages and by changing the phases, it continues without meter, like poetry, to get the extracts of the subjects, in order to build the big picture. Through this innovation, its solidly gathered subjects are able to inspire the vastness of any day's perception and at the same time the creation of brand-new songs, with different words or parts of the existing ones. The spectrum of the book to be expanded through selected qualitative music, which will spread its ideas with a wider width; from a guitar under a tree, till concerts with thousands spectators.

This treatise uses a method in which every word has a meaning, without research in an ocean, but with imminent effect, through intensive philosophy in an augmented process during Part A. Part B treats more basic issues, necessary to be mentioned. Both parts A and B are concluded in Part C.

Enjoy the invasion in the fundamental environment of self-realization, where the impossible is possible.

In life
what is not optional
it is
and what is optional
it isn't
because it must be proved
that you are not afraid of any today
to be capable of winning one tomorrow

Samples of structural components

The subjects are formed with the main bodies, the steps, the refrains, to be completed without meter.

(main body: part of 'The Idiosyncrasy of Whys', chapter 3)

The main direction is in the unanswered questions
in a rough and long distance without confirmations
guide-light to step foot in the beginning of forever
where willingness will be obliged to serve the soul

(main body: part of 'Borderless Eyes', chapter 5)

A tear falls when the wings just lift up only dust
but the barren earth needs even this tiny drop
as you need to be trained hard, to get stronger
to be prepared, because to fly needs duration

(step: part of 'Alarm-Clock', chapter 1)

Time is a healer and a wound
a knife pulled out, or pushed in
it depends on you, if the steam
on the mirror will say I love you

(Refrain: part of 'The Loyalty of Duty', chapter 4)

Armies against you
An army with you
An oath of principles

your destination
Make time to wonder
make time to count
and when you are there
you will know

   (without meter: part of 'Useful Fear', chapter 3)

The believed civilization
is on the wings of a mosquito
thrilled to find a swamp
to make its eggs
and drinks blood
to survive one more day
a process to make it forget
that it will be eaten
by the birds
to continue to warble

   (without meter: part of 'Parameters of Adjustment', chapter 2)

There is no they
when the ego
tries simulations in strangers' shoes
when the sight
looks lower than a midget's
when the pride
is abandoned like a whipped dog
then you
will be ignored as oxygen
the I to become a we

   (without meter: part of 'Nuances of Existence', chapter 5)

What faith doesn't want to genuflect
what love

doesn't want to hug
what hope
doesn't want efforts
what wish
doesn't want a destination
what purpose
doesn't want a reason
what life
doesn't want a meaning
the tears
to bring redemption

    (without meter: part of 'I am No One', chapter 4)

Morning vans full of papers
are picturing the new victims
especially in the first pages
Trains loaded with rumors
describing ships without sailors

    (without meter: part of 'Unsung Hero', chapter 1)

A leaf drops where it should be
Our only miracle is humanitarianism
our job is not to be a miracle any more

Samples of confirmation

The wider lines touch the limits of accessibility, when the purpose is every subject to be understood.

(part of 'Uncharted Waters')

Be afraid of the permanent which will become a predicted habit
is nothing else there than raw materials in strangers' ball of fibers
the time must weave the carpet with a variety of solved enigmas
to create the abilities one day to fly where you dared to imagine
because the real stability is the result of an unstoppable evolution

The difference between folded and unfolded text

(part of 'Restless Victory')

Serve your weaker brothers to give you the knowledge   *folded*
Reborn from your worst defeat and from your ashes win
Let cynicism hammer you like steel unbreakable to be
Then the war will be petrified the peace to be enforced

Serve your weaker brothers   *unfolded*
to give you the knowledge
Reborn from your worst defeat
and from your ashes win
Let cynicism hammer you like steel
unbreakable to be
Then the war will be petrified
the peace to be enforced

Mentality & Biometrics

The micro-technical philosophy expresses one entity, surrounds one mind, leaks from one society. It slides from family and friends in the neighborhood, the city, the country, to cultivate vertical* and horizontal* inside time the macro-technical philosophy which identifies our world; both sourced from the true truth to unleash the reasons. This philosophy is being addressed to you, because your actions can be decided from millions. When you follow the seemingly easy, many will do the same and it will become oppressive, to teach to the unapproachable; but if you are determined from your willingness, some will start to pursue the same path and the difficult will be no more. The ordinary acquires a mouth in the subject *'Divided Heroes',* to argue for its fears and to get answers from the choices. The book starts with what, for many, ends last, and through the guidelights of knowing themselves, leads them to kill it first; the unknown, to be known, the longest distance to be walked, by tracing the desires in the allurements of quintessence.

The book starts with what majorities think lasts longer

> Hope became the big lace fan of despair
> is cooling you in the frozen refrigerator
> of an artificially constructed happiness
> well dressed for the promiscuous ball

and almost ends with the pace which everyone can achieve,

                                    Kill first
                              what ends last
                                    the hope
                 to embrace the uncharted waters
                    and when the difficult times
                         unavoidably will come
                                not to abandon
                              not to surrender
                            not to die as a hero
                             but to live like one

to make life to happen.

Samples of micro-technical to macro-technical philosophy, in vertical*analysis to explore the level of needs for any entity to develop (mostly explains the ways for the small to grow) and horizontal* as the reckoning of majority's choices (usually in our societies is called they). For example: the less motivation for progress brings less chance for democracy, restricted in the balances between debts and prosperity.

Sample of vertical analysis, part of 'Seldom'

Everything started with a drop
which wanted to fill a pothole
and thought to become a lake
because it was determined to live

*Sample of vertical & horizontal analysis,
part of 'Biased Days'*

During the biased days don't ask for
justice, equality, rights or freedom
because you can't afford them at all

*Sample of horizontal & vertical analysis,
part of 'The Invisible Chain'*

just open your ears to listen
the clangs of the invisible chain
which bonds everyone's feet
is the orchestra which plays the music

*Sample of horizontal analysis,
part of 'The Fusion of Reaction'*

Our world is based on the economy
because you care about money
Our world focuses on the debts
because you like the easy ways
Our world sees the mathematics
because you don't want to contribute
Our world sends you the bill
because you don't take responsibilities

If this question has existence: Are the robots able to replace humans? Or are humans becoming robots?

*Sample of an answer out of many
part of 'Equilibrium'*

Comfortable the story in the glass
pendulum with happy endings
with rent the owned door
it doesn't open when you want

*Sample of an answer out of many
part of 'Paper-skin'*

Adults with mechanical moves
once used to be enough successful
to lose every sense of flexibility
easy to be replaced from robots

*Sample of an answer out of many
part of 'Calculus'*

Opinion without access
or access without opinion
ventriloquists' voices on mimes
a spectacle without protagonists

> *Sample of an answer out of many*
> *part of 'Dogma of Menace'*

Machines can replace only machines not humans
but the incapacity to develop emotional intelligence
and to progress also your authenticity
makes you function like a mechanism
able only to be evaluated from a particular efficiency
to fill up yourself inside boxes with predicted results
and our necessary evolution to be exposed in front of the eyes
of wars and women

In General Terms

What chances
has the arrogance of nothing

blindfolded from empty digits
against
the intelligence of creation

The alternative
doesn't choose particular names
the fantasy
to have no borders
the tears
to have no barriers
the happiness
to have no boundaries
the wishes
to have no barricades
because

freedom can't be given

must be earned

Only on a blank cheque
can sign
the ink of trust
where priceless
can't be bothered
from papers
where love
can't be forgotten
where friendship
offers both shoulders
to the broken legs
till they walk again

First the soul goes out
and then faith
which means
that if you are not
ready to die
for what you believe in
you never lived

The profound width of wisdom
makes us kneel from
real admiration
in front of the courtesy of its
magnificence
without dependences or orders
any other submission is just nickels

Modus Vivendi & Modus Operandi

PART A

The prisoners with open doors
(Surrounding Title)

Chapter One
Character: comprehension

The Decay of Hope

Hope became the big lace fan of despair
is cooling you in the frozen refrigerator
of an artificially constructed happiness
well dressed for the promiscuous ball

To light many candles, doesn't make the faith,
but the difficult footsteps in the depth of actions
Infidelity is not only to kill, to lie or to steal, but
also to throw in the garbage a bone with the skin

When hope is flapping without flagstaff
doesn't need air but emptiness

For how long you will raise your fist
only for someone else's victory?

Hope less to gain more
stable steps on the snow

A dance with the decadence   *(Refrain)*
the vibrations crack the beams
Just to breathe
Just to be
Just to exist

Life sourced from long-waiting wishes
is looking at the tide taking them away
again and again and again
till promises will be forgotten
Incomplete moments as a lifetime

Hope became the bridal hair of Dulcinea
insanity to be a faithful trust under a dome
moving sand to appear as a swimming pool
worked without spade, built without tiles

The swearing-in doesn't make the knight
but the hard work for the modesty of honor
functional edges don't need sharp blades
but strong belief beyond static existences

When hope is resurrected from empty digits
doesn't need elegance but shadow

For how long you will clap your hands
only for someone else's dignity?

Hope for nothing to gain everything
chisel to sculpture the soul

A dance with the decadence *(Refrain)*
the vibrations crack the beams
Just to breathe
Just to be
Just to exist
Life sourced from long-waiting wishes
is looking at the tide taking them away
again and again and again
till promises will be forgotten
Incomplete moments as a lifetime

Dedication is melting the bars of injustice
and there is no pact between lion and men
the victims of compromises will be defeated
incompetent the submissive pyramid of excuses

When hope is born from someone else's signature
doesn't need baby's cot but shelter

For how long you will lower your eyes
from a perfect life?

What about
the things you want to do; the different places to be
the crossed look through refined beauties
the vision of the dream you used to be
the inner challenges of expression
the hidden powers of devotion
the inspirations you admired
the senses you desired

Hope for the world not for you
when you have done your best
a fresh air in the lungs

The sun even behind heavy black clouds
constantly is waiting for a new tomorrow

A dance with the decadence *(Refrain)*
the vibrations crack the beams
Just to breathe
Just to be
Just to exist

Life sourced from long-waiting wishes
is looking at the tide taking them away
again and again and again
till promises will be forgotten
Incomplete moments as a lifetime

Alarm Clock

The easier of the old still a cloak inside a t-shirt
written on played-out banners of dim memories
protest among alliances with different denture
adaptations of the nothings of any suitable belief

Redundant emission for the eyes not to meet
unwritten amendments inside a vast mediocrity
the world's libraries shouldn't be enough for you
plaster all experiences, the back to avoid a hump

Time is a healer and a wound
a knife pulled out, or pushed in
it depends on you, if the steam
on the mirror will say I love you

Broken watches on the marbles *(Refrain)*
knowledge of fragments
the unborn wisdom
inspire the womb of civilization
possibilities countless
solutions priceless
to desire the impossible, a pledge
Commitments of confession

Scepters for those who can't shine without
countless coals for those who can innovate
the smudges paint two lines on every cheek
not a tear or a drop of sweat to be wasted

The seasons change because majorities don't
only marshes feel comfortable with stagnation
always the pioneers spit blood for the obvious
the countdown has started before you are born

The time is lost inside a non-baptized habit,
somewhere between Sunday and Monday
mortified the unbelievably humiliated hours
harmed from the incredible absence of quality

Broken watches on the marbles   *(Refrain)*
knowledge of fragments
the unborn wisdom
inspire the womb of civilization
possibilities countless
solutions priceless
to desire the impossible, a pledge
Commitments of confession

The future is today
a second passed already
the tin will be expired to become
the only nutrition for mad illusions

The new our preservation, rehabilitation, salvation
inauguration, affiliation, extension, consultation
our only destination in an accurate dimension
Without it, there is no tomorrow
nothing else can rescue us
but it will rise only
if you let it, if you hope for it
if you earned it, if you love it
if you deserve it, if you search it
if you advise it, if you warn for it
if you praise it, if you promise it

and then want and want more
and then want more

The alarm clock useful far before
the dialogue to be dried
the answers to be buried
the questions to be sunk
the words to be drowned

Broken watches on the marbles *(Refrain)*
knowledge of fragments
the unborn wisdom
inspire the womb of civilization
possibilities countless
solutions priceless
to desire the impossible, a pledge
Commitments of confession

and then want and want more
and then want more

Time is a healer and a wound
it depends on you, if the steam
on the mirror will say I love you

The First from the End

The nails embedded to climb on the jobless honesty
The breath can't stand this world but is getting stronger
The hands of sand are crumbling before pulling each other
The nakedness makes you choose a leaf than a bond

Without bait the fish-hook and wet with salted water
when you are thirsty

Intelligence and intellectuality not the fire exit
but the main gate

Polished gears when function on the opposite side
pack of cards wait for the wind

By groping you will start touching
Even for the first from the end
the fair can give the order for an about-turn in a huge parade
don't cross the red line

Stalactites down   *(Refrain)*
stalagmites up
the suitable visibility
Hard the nest of clay
with a peculiar sound
never heard before
music of determination
in a crowded isolation

The hands bruised to push the unemployed integrity
is not a door to open, but stones to remain unswerving
Backs of sand are crumbling before support each other
The velvet curtain makes you see the outside not the inside

The dead-end wishes with crystal bricks or Plexiglas
have the same boundaries

The small fish can hide from the big, but the boats
won't search for both

Steam train even for the opponent without wagons
at least to understand the distance

By whispering you will start talking
Even for the first from the last
faith can push the button for the last floor
in a grounded elevator
don't change confession

Stalactites down *(Refrain)*
stalagmites up
the suitable visibility
Hard the nest of clay
with a peculiar sound
never heard before
music of determination
in a crowded isolation

Responsibility is not a torch to hand over in a relay race
but a necessary marathon

Fireproof utensil the naked truth
touched or untouched is unbreakable
perpetual but announced as new
the naphthalene can't inspire passion

Nothing is imminent, nothing is easy
the code of contacts without discrimination
the code of ethics without observation
the code of senses without destination

Life is tough, to be improved
to reanimate new technicalities
to reconstruct new realities
to resurrect new societies
to rehabilitate old brutalities
to reinvent new logicalities
till The Carpenter becomes bald

The last will be first and the first last
upside down and from down to up
all our efforts across the centuries
are reminding us who we really are

Stalactites down *(Refrain)*
stalagmites up
the suitable visibility
Hard the nest of clay
with a peculiar sound
never heard before
music of determination
in a crowded isolation

Calculus

In a drawer the most famous fortune teller
when it opens she wakes up to tell the news
initiatives humbled in a spoiled public cynicism
improvisations forgotten in teenage thoughts
to share anything just became impossible

When the source is not from a gut feeling
bottle with holes hunts drops of sea water
unnoticed merciless eyes are always watching
the purposed ignorance won't stand for long
bucketfuls on the beach can't build high walls

The noise from the beans
which slide on the table
the temptation of tomorrow
vigilance just to be tired in the morning

Protractors can't map out life   *(Refrain)*
but obsessive certainties
which never came
Immature the incentives of nothing
just Sanskrit transcript in the agenda
The bulimic lies
always dizzy
to feel like truth

Paper numbers the most reliable prophets
sliced pieces in the fireplace to warm the day
individuality is handcuffed for harassment
the motive, a miracle, happened years ago
contribution an ammunition of vulnerability

The past is a river and the future a desert
time a game for the moon and the sun
but a tool to make you stronger, wiser
quicker, better for faithful fulfillments
or routine of hamster's wheel near a boa

Opinion without access
or access without opinion
ventriloquists' voices on mimes
a spectacle without protagonists

Protractors can't map out life   *(Refrain)*
but obsessive certainties
which never came
Immature the incentives of nothing
just Sanskrit transcript in the agenda
The bulimic lies
always dizzy
to feel like truth

Without pure sweat you are in a stranger's fields
why put your arms in someone else's sleeves?
when you are not the substitute but the prototype
calculus will be activated sooner or later, anyway

Carry on your shoulders the loaded cart
Push the wagon with your own two hands
Run the thousand stairs without the elevator
Knock the hundred doors without excuses
Swollen throat the actions you did, not tried

How secure do you feel with a foreign story?
When you wish what everybody wishes
When you know what everybody knows
When you see what everybody sees
When you do what everybody does
When no one else can save you
who is going to tell you?
Nothing is obvious

Diamonds the popular silence of the exact same failure
World is a slot-machine when the greater good is for free
Professionalism trained to hit the crossbars than to score
Nobody ordered you not to do or live as you really please
you did, in your calculations, the sum of your own quotient

Protractors can't map out life *(Refrain)*
but obsessive certainties
which never came
Immature the incentives of nothing
just Sanskrit transcript in the agenda
The bulimic lies
always dizzy
to feel like truth

Biased Days

When priority is the knot of the shoelace
is like head-rope slips fast on open palms
bandages can cover the figure of the soul
the wounds can heal with or without scars
but the anchor will disappear forever

Innocence can't be lost in teenage dreams
or in the shadows of wrinkled transactions
you are naive if you think you don't need
its wild nature to consciously protect you
not to be the victim in a parody of a circus

Where were you yesterday?
and the day before?
Where will you be tomorrow?
and the day after?

The borrowed body *(Refrain)*
bill before dawn
Groundless grounds
for a week or a century
just call them
the biased days
to move forward
and come back no more

The successful efficiency is not a jukebox
on hills of seaweed ready to be consumed
but the sparks of two stones to make fire
paper planes rarely asked for their design
lack like an extracted chord from a violin

The genocide of oppressive conservations
praise the death of the vouchers of defiance
to push the same button can't change a thing
just brings the cauldrons to boil our lethal future
with the exact same taste as the biased days

Were you in an exotic place or familiar?
more than you know
The incidents which happened already
are not surprises any more

The borrowed body *(Refrain)*
bill before dawn
Groundless grounds
for a week or a century
just call them
the biased days
to move forward
and come back no more

During the biased days don't ask for
justice, equality, rights or freedom
because you can't afford them at all

Without effort there is no redemption
To risk or not is a decision, not a choice
To be or not somewhere else tomorrow
To seize or not what can belong to you

Ineffective the silence of breath
just to forget what is not obvious
lost in the sound of familiarity
kidnapped without brutality
surrendered without immortality
just to witness the similarity
with the day before and the day after

There is no luck to experience
a future wedged inside it
is just the fog on the scene
kneeled to feel like walking
not to go anywhere else
not to see something new
not to love someone ugly
not to choose an avalanche for duty
not to guide the away
far, far from today

The borrowed body *(Refrain)*
bill before dawn
Groundless grounds
for a week or a century
just call them
the biased days
to move forward
and come back no more

Unsung Hero

The mask of apathy absorbs the name
Determination in shadows of sarcasm
To empower the crystal innocent eyes
Trembled steps forward should be enforced
Even the way of the ant mustn't be bothered

A prisoner with the open door
The seasons change just once
from the old years to the new
Fight with greatest and worst
To win everything or nothing

Prevention to confront clepsydras of fire
but a month before uninvited for supper
a year before unforgivable from societies
a decade before prehistoric for moments

Words of stone *(Refrain)*
combined all dictionaries
Light before the end of the corridor
the vision is the mission
unstoppable force
to break any wall
till the sacrifices of today
dominate tomorrow

The spirit ripped the skin to speak
put two mirrors on the head to see
the efforts created the ears to listen
The body of temptations an enemy and a friend
muscles on the soul the actions you can't regret

David and Goliath in a perpetual war
The most passionate warrior will win
A fear of death shouldn't be a threat
The silence of loneliness a great lover
Confident to crack statues with a myth

Sadness and happiness bonded with tears
to discover the recipe, an unseen feeling
wonderful the flavor to influence the rest
without tasting the technicalities of deception

Words of stone   *(Refrain)*
combined all dictionaries
Light before the end of the corridor
the vision is the mission
unstoppable force
to break any wall
till the sacrifices of today
dominate tomorrow

No weekends, no vacations, no days off
To move or not a chess piece, is a choice
Publicity is important for serious matters
useless when you can have all without it
Is difficult to identify a true unsung hero
because his fist raises with thousands others
to see his biography impossible when you live in it

Cause and effect
without negotiations
without compromises
without tolerance
consensus is unnecessary
only cement and steel
for greater foundations
for us and the coming generations

What clothes to wear
when skeleton bodies are covered with flies
How much water to use
when a drop is priceless for millions
How much food to eat
when sacks of rice keep alive entire nations
For how long will you be passenger
in the common sense of a jeopardized future?

A leaf drops where it should be
Our only miracle is humanitarianism
our job is not to be a miracle any more

Words of stone *(Refrain)*
combined all dictionaries
Light before the end of the corridor
the vision is the mission
unstoppable force
to break any wall
till the sacrifices of today
dominate tomorrow

Guardian of justice by your side
a prisoner with the open door
light before the end of the corridor
no one to walk in the dark any more
with one voice through eternity

Unknown Nature

I learned to live with grey and blue
in your possession the other colors
ray with a quick glance on the road
only the two of us know, no one else
is not just a gear to fit, but far more

Your beauty can make legions to knell
if sourced from intuition not insecurity
You are born capable to confront a lion
I want all your senses even for one night
I don't care for less, you shouldn't either

Don't tell me why
I want to comprehend you, muted yes
Don't tell me how
I will send you flowers on an ordinary day

Flawless No   *(Refrain)*
the sharpest edge known
till you are certain
and then no again
to become a woman
and make me a man
I am afraid of you
because I love you

Your body is my temple, water in the desert
Your liberation my oxygen, breath of fresh air
Your curves a trip without return, my horizon

I can't take my eyes off you, endless sea
This natural devoted addiction can destroy me

I have to sacrifice your feelings stronger to be
To learn more of your pure unknown nature
and meet your perfection on the next corner
Just make me miss you, not to forget you,
waiting a ghost doesn't make the man you want

Don't tell me when
I will come to find you and protect you
Don't tell me where
select the table, I will choose the chair

Flawless No   *(Refrain)*
the sharpest edge known
till you are certain
and then no again
to become a woman
and make me a man
I am afraid of you
because I love you

I am begging you
walk, talk, act, smile, think, dream, feel
like a woman to become one
to gain the uniqueness of your femininity
to give you my innocence to hold
There is no other trust to ask
but the magnets of chemistry
no loops can confirm passion
we are not mammals in a flock
the battle of egoism is hard
your freedom to become mine too

Request the moon
in the middle of the ocean
and I will ask for a dance on it
to run again and find you
holy game in a vicious world
which I will change because of you
just be better than my imagination
be the real you, with the sight of a woman

You are my first obstacle
to teach me how to love
be tough
be soft
be wild
be tender
don't be gentle
just be you

and if I lose you
let the sunset to remind you

Flawless No   *(Refrain)*
the sharpest edge known
till you are certain
and then no again
to become a woman
and make me a man
I am afraid of you
because I love you

Please take me home
I need your smell to protect me
This emotional touch will never end
The simplicity of complexity counts the most

The Journey

I will construct a small boat with two oars
splinters to know what every finger can do
calluses to touch the sad and happy equally
all experiences are precious and saltiness
makes the skin thicker for unwise criticisms

First the two thirds and then the rest
the vast sea in the land's possibilities
to know myself and then all the world
to see the similarity before the news
to learn what life is, not to imagine it

Helm for the ports
where the welcomes will be warmer
where the handkerchiefs will wave longer

Shipwrecks made the ocean liners *(Refrain)*
from wood to steel
pieces at almost every rock
fatalities for a divergent view
to build anew or to abandon
but I don't care to survive
I don't need a shelter
I want to live

Thin sail to become rags with the first wind
to learn the language of small and big fishes
to teach them about the nets and the hooks
that bait is never enough, safety till the coast
to meet a true friend to help me walk again

Don't see castaway's clothes but the quality
without adventures the pedestrians from life
problems in shop windows like theirs concern others
plastic securities with continuous devaluations
butter and tea even with forty-five degrees

Anchor for the ports
where hugs won't be just for one day
where understanding will never forget me

Shipwrecks made the ocean liners *(Refrain)*
from wood to steel
pieces at almost every rock
fatalities for a divergent view
to build a new or to abandon
but I don't care to survive
I don't need a shelter
I want to live

You have to miss everything
to comprehend what really matters the most
You have to lose all materials
to understand that you never needed them
You have to be hungry
the food to be more tasty than you know
You have to get thirsty
the water to be more refreshing than ever

Time does and doesn't exist
just a clepsydra which turns
till the rain stops
till the snow melts
till the fruit ripens

You can't build a lifetime by following what shines
you need a sinking boat to become better than yesterday
to discover the extension of your palms to take the water out
not to underestimate your mind and voice by watching big ships
even the perfect days don't have the same value tomorrow
even the most expensive stones need to be restructured
because even the richest stagnation is expendable

My boat has a name and a soul
no one can take it from me
My heritage
a broken piece of wood
wet from a thousand seas

Shipwrecks made the ocean liners *(Refrain)*
from wood to steel
pieces at almost every rock
fatalities for a divergent view
to build a new or to abandon
but I don't care to survive
I don't need a shelter
I want to live

A journey without ticket

Restricted Districts

The extempore water well is the marbled fountain
in a different square
The wooden talisman is the golden necklace
at a different address

What difference does it make to lie
for a crumb or a bread?
the bakery is the same
when the dough could have been exquisite

Without your unique offer
don't expect something
I can destroy you
if I will do what you did
if I will think as you think

Someone has to lose   *(Refrain)*
and it is going to be you
Doomed or virtual life
the same prison
Reasons count, not excuses
the syllabus is simple
the tooth under the pillow
is not useful any more

The vouchers for mess allowance are the caviar with champagne
in a different neighborhood
The clothes in shop baskets are the bureaucratic suits
with different tags

What difference does it make to beg
for a hut or a palace?
the compromise is the same
when the sweat could have been familiar

Without your new contribution
don't ask for anything
I can humiliate you
if I don't see what you should have watched
if I don't hear what you should have listened

Someone has to lose *(Refrain)*
and it is going to be you
Doomed or virtual life
the same prison
Reasons count, not excuses
the syllabus is simple
the tooth under the pillow
is not useful any more

Numbers against numbers
Shadows against shadows
Greed against greed
Rich against poor
Well buried the same secret
in the exact same box
with different wrapping paper
clash for the colored ribbon
someone else to blame
undeclared war
in an unwritten law

Even if you are homeless
someone will need your help
Even if you are the boss
someone will give you orders

Ambitious new boxers always wait

I will treat you as you treated the weaker
I will salute you as you saluted the stronger
To help you act as you should have acted
To make you live as you should have lived
To be better first for yourself and then for the rest
You can't confront me
I am invisible
I am your faith
you should have kowtowed
in front of me, years ago
do it now, before it's too late
because I am you

Someone has to lose *(Refrain)*
and it is going to be you
Doomed or virtual life
the same prison
Reasons count, not excuses
the syllabus is simple
the tooth under the pillow
is not useful any more

Restricted districts
in will
Restricted districts in belief
Restricted districts in imagination
Restricted districts in life's incarnation
Restricted districts
the place we never chose to be

Voice in the Crowd

In every home will be served the truth
everyone to get drunk from happiness
straight walk on the line with open arms
responsibility to be kissed in every corner

Maturity will ask you what you want
your inspiration's a precious element
the gravity of dignity always present
productive integrity the only account

Don't wait for any when
Which drop in the ocean wave can be stopped?
can sculpt any rock
Climb, because you can

FORWARD! *(Refrain)*
We walk in the rain
inside the thick mud
FORWARD!
We blow up to the sky
the clouds to go away
FORWARD!
One and another one
and another one and another one
to finally see the sun
The new Era has begun

The diamond rings to help the well-paid miners
the part-timers open the new road of education
all the people find their own real destination
The oasis doesn't have feet to find the caravans

Tents only to be closer to Mother Nature
to listen the apologies of the mosquitoes
they had to warn even on idyllic beaches
garbage will feed the wished immoral power

Don't wait to be represented
Which expression of the heart can be gagged?
words always be respected
Speak, because you can

FORWARD! *(Refrain)*
We walk in the rain
inside the thick mud
FORWARD!
We blow up to the sky
the clouds to go away
FORWARD!
One and another one
and another one and another one
to finally see the sun
The new Era has begun

The biggest revolutions weren't lethal
not to be understood, but to be lived
The grass will always need to be watered

The one can make the difference
but all fingers must gather for victory
to totally demolish the ifs and maybes
same bricks to start the temple of our will
Labyrinth with mirrors for those who left behind

Which order can stop a dream?
Which pledge can stop a whisper?
Which irony can stop existence?
Which arid land doesn't want a river?
Which night doesn't need the stars?
Which thought will make you come?
One and another one and another one

Don't wait for promises
Which hand doesn't want to lift you up?
just to pray is not enough
acts of proof without fear
Risk, because you can

FORWARD! *(Refrain)*
We walk in the rain
inside the thick mud
FORWARD!
We blow up to the sky
the clouds to go away
FORWARD!
One and another one
and another one and another one
to finally see the sun
The new Era has begun

Which freedom keeps the keys?
The voice in the crowd can be yours
can be mine, can be anyone's and everyone's
If I can do it, you can do it, we all can do it
and then it will be easy, an everyday life
Another one and another one and another one
The new Era has begun!

The Stairs

What to count
when the deep wrinkle wants to hear itself
I am afraid to be jealous of it

What to count
when the words of efforts find their meaning
to be understood and respected

What to count
when hunger ends with trembled hands through fingers
and thirst with wet chest

What to count
when the deepest grief of sadness finds a smile
is the shiniest sunshine

What to count
when one became more than a thousand
when I saw your beauty

Which minute is a lifetime?
Which lifetime is a minute?
What to count
when I met you

Precious the under-construction building's stairs   *(Refrain)*
even if it has one chance
just one chance
to become a house

One more tear
one more touch
one more word
one more step
higher than yesterday
lower than tomorrow
Only the tinny hearts have limits

What to count
when a big full basket is loaded on the shoulders of a very old woman
how much costs every step?

What to count
when the hand of a destroyed body after decades of defeat
is still searching for the ropes of the ring

What to count
when just a calendar doesn't propose the dance any more
but even a very rainy day

What to count
when a barren land becomes a huge granary
and only one seed is mine

What to count
when I didn't know even how to walk
and now I can run

Which moment is eternity?
Which eternity is a moment?
What to count
when I met me

Precious the under-construction building's stairs   *(Refrain)*
even if it has one chance
just one chance
to become a house
One more tear
one more touch
one more word
one more step
higher than yesterday
lower than tomorrow
Only the tinny hearts have limits

Free will
the widest canyon
Life trains us with what we can count
to live it with what we cannot

Which level of sacrifice you can afford?
The eyes can adapt the darkness
to think that you are able to see
when you don't
The ears can be used to fake compliments
to believe that you hear everything
when you can't
Only the pain of truth
can wake up the senses
to make them stronger
to let you feel broken emotions
the only way to gain the lust
to love

Every cent of greed
is empting your own lake
which has been given
to find and fulfill your visions
by walking to flying

Dreams are only in the sleep
But if you waste the water around
the friendships won't last
privileges will become rags
reputation will be mud
till you find the source
to fill it up
Even one drop of wisdom
is enough

Can be counted
one kilo of tomatoes
debts and profits
Quest to find the victims

Nothing can lift you up
when the wounds of the soul
don't care to heal
but to forget

Precious the under-construction building's stairs   *(Refrain)*
even if it has one chance
just one chance
to become a house
One more tear
one more touch
one more word
one more step
higher than yesterday
lower than tomorrow
Only the tinny hearts have limits

What to count
when the dirtiest clothes
can't stop a hug

Step up, step down
here is the pathway
paradise or underground
earthen-road or mainstream
Decision for Judgment Day

Unswerving

How many pieces with a concealed embalmed truth
gagged and locked behind closed doors
because even undernourished is immortal
can assemble to build the picture of the future?

Your eyes can't look in a different direction at the same time
Find yourself, to find myself
to find everybody
unswerving to be
as chorus
as melody
as harmony
as history

What keeps you awake?
What lets you to sleep?
Is it something different
or a surrealistic possibility

Impulse to pulses   *(Refrain)*
pulses to impulse
identical frequency
Shell of coal
sparks to fire
to unleash the shape
the figure of spirit
Unswerving faith

How many wishes infected with consumption
to give opium to the body in a coma
and oxygen for fake hopes of survival
can bring the necessary changes for prosperity?

Your feet can't be stable by standing on two boats for long
Find your disadvantages, to find my advantages
to find the ideology
unswerving to be
as friend
as society
as union
as world

What keeps you silent?
What makes you scream?
Is it something peculiar
or a supernatural scene

Impulse to pulses   *(Refrain)*
pulses to impulse
identical frequency
Shell of coal
sparks to fire
to unleash the shape
the figure of spirit
Unswerving faith

How many alibis can mesmerize the vital need for inner changes?
How many pieces can be missed to see the image of a puzzle?
How many wishes must be totally swept to clear the big picture?
How many decisions were in favor of you without your presence?
How many missions have succeeded without believing in them?

Can you stop thinking yourself?
to start loving it
Can you forget every yesterday?
to be alive today
Can you ignore any incomplete joy?
to be happy tomorrow
Can you blame yourself for someone else's fault?
to be unswerving

By waiting on the queue
because is crowded
you just buy an excuse
not to avoid the trap

Even the healthiest addiction
unsuspectingly blindfolds the sight
the unfamiliar to be familiar
Different honor inside you
different honor outside you
Which one will prevail?
to be unswerving
as a whole and as a being
the same thing
in a smaller screen
the entire world
is reflecting your every move
boomerangs learn from you
to know how to teach you

The body is recording every mistake
every kilometer in a wrong path
will create cellular whispers
starting with gossips
which will become reality

Impulse to pulses *(Refrain)*
pulses to impulse
identical frequency
Shell of coal
sparks to fire
to unleash the shape
the figure of spirit
Unswerving faith

You saw what I didn't
you know what I don't
you touch what I won't
unswerving we can promise
nothing to be unknown

Equilibrium

The will abandoned in time-shelve
cobwebs from the total lack of light
thick dust from the absence of air
the ashes of the memory
not to remember the flowing river

Comfortable the story in the glass
pendulum with happy endings
with rent the owned door
it doesn't open when you want

Riders of the same fantasy
Somewhere
Sometime
The languid words to make a phrase

To serve a need   *(Refrain)*
is slavery
To serve ambition
immaturity
To serve inspiration
justice
Nothing can be bought
everything must be earned
in one way or another
the seesaw must touch the ground

Desires oppressed in a dripping tap
the last noise in pleasurable habits
before the pipes of imagination rust
to let the ears unaware to sleep
to leave the age without protection shield

Songs with a stranger's happiness
navigated for known places
lost in empty horoscopes
distorted thoughts in photo albums

Guardians of the same dream
Somehow
Someday
Fake smiles to start laughing

To serve a need *(Refrain)*
is slavery
To serve ambition
immaturity
To serve inspiration
justice
Nothing can be bought
everything must be earned
in one way or another
the seesaw must touch the ground

Where are the limits of confrontation?
in communication without understanding
in credibility without reckoning
in reductions without quests
in answers without questions

By reading someone else's pages
no matter how many they are
is not your sweat
is not your inspiration
is not your income
is just a boost
if you decide to live

By following someone else's orders
no matter how dirty are the hands
is not your work
is not your prayer
is not your oath
is just a choice
to wake you up

By depending on someone else's deal
no matter how many shelters you have
is not your recognition
is not your revelation
is not your distinction
is just a fairy tale
to break your dreams

You gave up everything
just to gain lame excuses
but for whom?
Who will buy
patience for pity?

To serve a need   *(Refrain)*
is slavery
To serve ambition
immaturity
To serve inspiration
justice

Nothing can be bought
everything must be earned
in one way or another
the seesaw must touch the ground

I am nothing
nothing more than everything

Chapter Two
Character: intensive

Seldom

Everything started with a drop
which wanted to fill a pothole
and thought to become a lake
because it was determined to live

But had to push an irresolute wall
without listening to the impossible
but it was devoted to demolishing it
to define new norms for respect

Don't hear what the others say
just look
the eyes which never even tried
and eat
the tasty products of your spirit

Everything started with a word   *(Refrain)*
which wanted to be a song
Not punished from the music
not misjudged from the lyrics
not abused from the singer
but surrounded as unique
Not for someone else
but for itself

Everything started with an idea
which wanted to go against the river
it didn't count if the depth was too deep
because it had to learn how to swim

But had to confront jobless obstacles
and it decided to totally destroy them
it didn't even care to gain recognition
but to make one further step for you

Don't see what the others do
just notice
the decay of their stagnation
and drink
the thirst of your heart and soul

Everything started with a word *(Refrain)*
which wanted to be a song
Not punished from the music
not misjudged from the lyrics
not abused from the singer
but surrounded as unique
Not for someone else
but for itself

The station was always empty
the train has passed already
don't wait for another to come
it will never be the real one
because someone has to run faster

Even the steepest peak
wants to be seen
it will give you the pickaxe
to open a small path
and to become an earth-road

willing to be asphalted
to show the perfection of the landscape
it preserves for so many years

You shouldn't worry
the wounds will drive you there
because they want to heal

The fake limits end
when the real limits start
a hundred times longer
To reach the unreachable
not necessarily as the initiation imagined
not unavoidably to succeed
but to open new owned doors
the spirit to control the flesh
to seize every lust of impossible
and to avoid
the body to control the mind
to be addicted
with an ice-cream ball in the winter

Everything started with a word *(Refrain)*
which wanted to be a song
Not punished from the music
not misjudged from the lyrics
not abused from the singer
but surrounded as unique
Not for someone else
but for itself

Everything started with a look
destined to become strong feelings
but feared to dive into the emotions
to discover the destination of love
loneliness not to be alone in the rare pathways

Invisible Chain

The sunbeam entered the room
the eyes wanted to move the body
forced it to hold the unfriendly iron
they were delighted to see more

One of the most perfect views
the yellow grass of the valley
which was no one's property
took a promise to get watered

When real men are defined by smashing any obstacle
the problems will not endure
When passionate women search for spirituality
orgasms will turn the world around

One step of yours *(Refrain)*
two steps of mine
achievements to be lived
history to cry without victims
redemption will not be convicted
when traffic jams will search for it
with passion

The time forgot the minutes
barely remembered hours
scores on the wall counts
the days and the months

A photograph, the best friend
which acquired flesh and blood
the past to seem like a myth
because there is no tomorrow

When hunger will be considered in every poor or rich diner
the clouds will make us the favor
When bribery will not be accepted, will not be offered
and corruption will not rot the world

One step of yours *(Refrain)*
two steps of mine
achievements to be lived
history to cry without victims
redemption will not be convicted
when traffic jams will search for it
with passion

You shouldn't be a prisoner
to search for freedom
You shouldn't be a millionaire
to enjoy a wish
You shouldn't be a clown
to bring a smile
You shouldn't be a hero
to enforce justice
But as an ordinary person
just praise life

Just a seed in one side will become a garden in the other
a glass of water will become champagne
a morsel will become an extra dessert
a t-shirt will become a dinner-jacket
a book will strengthen the voice on both sides

The imprisoned soul
don't let the feet
make a further step
in the diminished visibility
not for revenge
but is just a warning
like the body does
before a serious disease

One step of yours   *(Refrain)*
two steps of mine
achievements to be lived
history to cry without victims
redemption will not be convicted
when traffic jams will search for it
with passion

shshshshshshsh
just open your ears to listen
the clangs of the invisible chain
which bonds everyone's feet
is the orchestra which plays the music

Make the noise sound
one step back of yours will take all of us down
Can you carry our weight on the ground?

The clangs of the invisible chain   *(noise of clangs)*
The clangs of the invisible chain
The clangs of the invisible chain
The clangs of the invisible chain
The clangs of the invisible chain

Paper-skin

Competent the youth of sponge
to dive in the depths of happiness
paper-ships to encourage the waves
to float with vivid hopeful winds

But the skin is covering with paper
every cheek is desperate for a seal
strange the signatures of certainty
to declare the lost destination

The poison can kill
but can create a medicine to heal
The fire can burn
but can warm in the deadly frost
The coin has two sides

There is no documented amnesty *(Refrain)*
no paper or photo
can describe life
only the heart can
through the eyes
anything else, anything less
just a photocopy
of a cheap imitation

Adults with mechanical moves
once used to be enough successful
to lose every sense of flexibility
easily to be replaced from robots

The name survives only on a slab
hooded from the cheated desperation
The calendar commands the dates
when everybody is allowed to smile

The oxygen can bring rust
but gives the breath to live
The knowledge can be a weapon
but can be used as peaceful tool
The knife has two usages

There is no documented amnesty *(Refrain)*
no paper or photo
can describe life
only the heart can
through the eyes
anything else, anything less
just a photocopy
of a cheap imitation

When you touch the gold
doesn't mean you can have it
When you can carry it
doesn't mean it will be yours
When you talk about it
doesn't mean that gets value for you
When you can show it
doesn't mean that it will ever belongs to you

The dead time
is been paid
not to be noticed
with special gifts
shiny rattles
the noises to cover
what really matters

Only the body can be given
tenderness can't commit a sin
when the hopes are water
flowed for better days to come

A lost breath for a while
can't accelerate a serious crime
when actions are committed
to bring back a truthful smile

Who doesn't want to cry
by thinking the worst
Who doesn't want to smile
by thinking the best

There is no documented amnesty *(Refrain)*
no paper or photo
can describe life
only the heart can
through the eyes
anything else, anything less
just a photocopy
of a cheap imitation

Paper-skin to be believed
importance for the unimportant
Honesty is the best sleeping pill
to enlighten the life deeply
in the emotions of the modesty

Roots

The thought wrapped in a sheet
To sparkle the eyes
To traumatize the ordinary
To complete the breath
To hypnotize the pain

The idea is a voracious gigantic guardian
to energize the mind and eat the doubts
through every individual to save the world
But which contents of a black plastic bag
can believe a poor unknown prophet

The extempore ink
even if it barely writes
can sign for humanity

I am searching for redemption *(Refrain)*
not for resurrection
Ready to go anywhere
till I find home
where the limitless horizons
will be seen
not only from my own screen

The evolution warms in a nest
The new love to be loved
The pure landscape to be seen
The alternative to be unique
The obvious to be expired

The main part of the wave will remain
from crossing through the ship canal
the misbelievers will always abandon
But which ball of a confined roulette
believes in others' wider circles of life

The handmade cement
with faith of stainless steel
can support eternity

I am searching for redemption *(Refrain)*
not for resurrection
Ready to go anywhere
till I find home
where the limitless horizons
will be seen
not only from my own screen

The roots can't be seen
but must be found
to electrify the delayed truth
not the plausible lies
In a letter
which has never been written
A brook
which has never been flowed
A wish
which has never been told
A wind
which has never been blown
A chess game
which never finished

Everywhere clenched teeth
to be hooked like a tree
careless to gain the capacity
to produce oxygen of any kind

The beautiful is searching for the wild
to survive
The hard is searching for the soft
to decide
Women and men
the two extreme opposite poles
the satin textile is just the detail
some whispers in the middle
try to reduce the battlefields
the refugee to find the house

The raw beauty of the nature can't be ignored
can't be abandoned
can't be redundant
in a civilized world

I am searching for redemption *(Refrain)*
not for resurrection
Ready to go anywhere
till I find home
where the limitless horizons
will be seen
not only from my own screen

The roots are the thoughts, the ideas, the senses
The temporary belongings
exist to create new realities
But the drums of war never stop
Are you willing to fight?

The fear will come
just to be confronted
Don't be afraid
When God is with you
who can be against you

I am searching for redemption   *(Refrain)*
not for resurrection
Ready to go anywhere
till I find home
where the limitless horizons
will be seen
not only from my own screen

Parameters of Adjustment

We are all born with the back on the wall
no matter how full or empty is the wallet
in front, a wide-open spectrum of pleasures
but you can't get the satisfaction as you want

Sooner or later the compromises will come
guillotine for the time and then for the rest
again and again many invisible crossroads
which had to become four-lane highways

It's not easy
to bend
but it's more difficult
to stand

Strong the voices within   *(Refrain)*
wait no answers, no questions
because you know
The current actions for a cause
The discipline to fly
on your very own
without borders
every drop of purpose

The back starts to push the wall harder and harder
searching for the locked door of a new dimension
it doesn't really matter if it will be big or very small
because it's there where you always belonged

By rummaging you must find a raw piece of iron
by learning you will gain a rasp to sculpture it
to make every angle become the perfect key
to avoid watching all your life from a keyhole

It's not easy
to be enslaved
but it's more difficult
to be free

Strong the voices within *(Refrain)*
wait no answers, no questions
because you know
The current actions for a cause
The discipline to fly
on your very own
without borders
every drop of purpose

You have to experience unremitting Mondays
to finally meet a clear-minded Sunday
which you can never reach
till it finds you
don't be in a rush

By delivering favors
to climb in the hierarchy
is just to continue to offer them
with the back on a rocky mass
stable on the foot of the mountain
smiling by ignoring what matters
and waiting for the landslide to come

When reality will find you
even inside a grave
it would have been great luck
if you couldn't even buy a box
free to dig with your own two hands
to finally find home
as you always imagined
your nails will be dirty for a while
but the tenderness of truth
will protect you for ever

Love can't be restricted
to worship just a figure
it doesn't need to remember
it doesn't need to forget
to be alive
the sensitivity of a touch
to remain
without wearing gloves
not to leave a fingerprint
on a dusty consciousness

There is no they
when the ego
tries simulations in strangers' shoes
when the sight
looks lower than a midget's
when the pride
is abandoned like a whipped dog
then you
will be ignored as oxygen
the I to become a we

Strong the voices within   *(Refrain)*
wait no answers, no questions
because you know
The current actions for a cause
The discipline to fly
on your very own
without borders
every drop of purpose

Start digging

The Vision Beyond

Is not a work
to carry an existing need
but a coach without horses

You must make a sincere drilling
to invade deeper than you can
to find elixirs of independence
within crystal clear transparence
and if the blinkers are in fashion
the lips of the souls will be parched
to let you insist for the obvious

Strong walk forward in the mud
till it becomes a road
Throw heavy rocks in the rough sea
till it becomes a gulf

Stretch out your arms to catch a hope *(Refrain)*
and if you deserve it
it won't fly away
There are no sacrifices
to fulfill a vision
Casualties must be ignored
The only elements
victory or defeat
to be beyond
acknowledging
every day's eternity

Is not a job
to sell programmed goods
but a portrait without a face

You must thrust a plough-share deeper
in barren land with fertile will
the acquired needs to expand
every inch, a great new knowledge
every meter, an elegant fresh desire
the patience of unavoidable delays
to create a valley in the desert

Put a raft against the furious waves
till it becomes a ship
Dare to gaze constantly in the infinity
till it becomes a horizon

Stretch out your arms to catch a hope *(Refrain)*
and if you deserve it
it won't fly away
There are no sacrifices
to fulfill a vision
Casualties must be ignored
The only elements
victory or defeat
to be beyond
acknowledging
every day's eternity

The line which never met an end
which erased as a mistake
which burned to become ashes
which buried to decompose quicker
where a cactus planted on purpose
with long entanglements around
But without being possible

it jumped from the paper to a screen
because even in an unfinished line's last breaths
the vision beyond the trite
can survive

The past is a sweater which getting unpicked
warmed the winters it should have
but is running out of style
The thread is one entity
held tight from the fear
when the steps are walking the unknown
but the trembling hands
want to let it go
the wind to take it away
not to return back again
because they decided to live
to gain the chance
even with just a quick taste
even with just an instant touch
even with just a fleeting glance
to approach
the vision beyond

Stretch out your arms to catch a hope   *(Refrain)*
and if you deserve it
it won't fly away
There are no sacrifices
to fulfill a vision
Casualties must be ignored
The only elements
victory or defeat
to be beyond
acknowledging
every day's eternity

Even one simple crack
with the courage to imagine
can break the glass of the micro-world
to unleash the time from the virtual clepsydra
to start breathing free in the real world
to let the air refresh its sand
which streams down between the fingers
oriented to create a brand-new beach
while the satisfied eyes
are looking with fulfilled passion
the harmonic waves of the moonlight

Fatal Acceptance

In the name of humanity
cruel crimes have been committed
Exposed those who didn't adapt
the mass menace of a public limbo

Money wouldn't have had power
if slavery hadn't have been popular
Protests for the extra hole in the pocket
when freedom has been lost forever

Which happiness never ends?
Which luxury always shines?
The words have synonyms
to lie without lying

Choose one finger out of two *(Refrain)*
when you have another eight
Keep the eye closed to watch
who is going to prevail?
to proudly pretend
a fictitious victory
Fatal acceptance
of a mystery

Insidious eyes read announcements in public
arrogance of power the today's autographs
but the feet will lose the ground under them
when their signature will be used as firelighters

The dogs are running after a moving bone
nobody really cares if they are hungry
some laugh just at watching this action
and bet to confirm their own destruction

Which obsession can be defended?
Which addiction can be stabilized?
The tone changes the meaning
to smile without smiling

Choose one finger out of two   *(Refrain)*
when you have another eight
Keep the eye closed to watch
who is going to prevail?
to proudly pretend
a fictitious victory
Fatal acceptance
of a mystery

What about
all fists to rise in the same time?
What about
each eye to see without color blindness?
What about
the right hand to cooperate with the left?
What about
the one or the other ear not to wear an earplug?
What about
a tear for a total stranger
We all are different, till a sharp blade touches the skin

Lawless and lawful laws
are stretching the same rope
an invitation only for pliant waists
with the excuse of a necessary dance

and steep descents of partial exceptions
disguised in inauguration's ribbons
an ancient custom for the few
in the name of the people

In a mortal world
who is not a victim?
with or without a name
quarry or persecutor
but only the hunter knows
that doesn't exist such a thing
as a neutral way of living

Choose one finger out of two   *(Refrain)*
when you have another eight
Keep the eye closed to watch
who is going to prevail?
to proudly pretend
a fictitious victory
Fatal acceptance
of a mystery

Her hair is hiding the face   *(unavoidable passion)*
but not the beauty
not the eyes to betray the thoughts
while she is waiting for the hand
to comfort them behind her ear
to unleash the core of the feelings
for the ceremony of the fateful acceptance
where the vows shouldn't be forgotten
an initiation for just the one
which is aiming to expand
for all the rest

Ignition

Everyone is a recipient of many great gifts
straws dispersed to be found and gathered
tie in a sheaf, not the wind to take them away
clean to float on the ocean and to be saved
from the whales not to worry for the sharks

From water in the middle of the depth of the sea
pipes still provide the survival, not to dive deeper
comfortable boxes teach to be afraid of the bottom
but weakened muscles can't cherish your own ignition
to swim from the darkness to the light
To see the surface of a new beginning
To visualize the horizon you imagined

Whisper silently a brand-new song
which maybe no one will sing

Burn fire burn   *(Refrain 1)*
burn my senses
till the end
Progress your own dimensions
to justify any ignition
innovation, inspiration, improvisation, implementation,
Affiliation
without hierarchical discrimination

The choice is hard and flexible like iron
can be transmuted in a slipshod crown
to give the illusion of absolute freedom
or in merciless chains to pinion both legs
because you have to try again, till you do

Every morning alleges to bring brand new days
but the road remembers what you want to forget
the tires didn't become the extension of your feet
traffic jams offer the decision for your own ignition
Traffic lights stop you, to think it over
to gain the chance of alternative ways
to focus on your desires not the musts

Walk even barefooted in an isolated path
where maybe no one will follow

Burn fire burn   *(Refrain 1)*
burn my senses
till the end
Progress your own dimensions
to justify any ignition
innovation, inspiration, improvisation, implementation,
Affiliation
without hierarchical discrimination

Hollow sound the reputation
thunder with a strong flash
pierces with light the darkest sky
can't be seen where it hits
but everybody knows that exists

Food for curiosity the rumors
are trying to fly without wings
to walk on the clouds
which will never taste
the nectar of rain

Give everything you got
it's all that matters
do only the right thing
to enforce justice
even if you are the only one
and the entire world
will celebrate the day
that lambs became lions
without asking for rights
but possess them
stood on their own two feet
to reveal the real revolution
No more favors
just foundations of actions

Burn fire burn   *(Refrain 1)*
burn my senses
till the end
Progress your own dimensions
to justify any ignition
innovation, inspiration, improvisation, implementation,
Affiliation
without hierarchical discrimination

Can you be a deserter from the flesh
to discover the spirit?
Can you afford to sacrifice yourself
for just a half step forward?
to inspire others to do the rest?
to endure the continuous rejection?

But if you do
before the end
you will be certain
that you didn't spend your life in vain

Burn fire burn *(Refrain 2)*
burn my senses
till the end
Give everything you got
it's all that matters
No more favors
just foundations of justice

The Autopsy of Rejection

With belts is pinioned the back
to pull the weight of tomorrow
the pain is the prelude of wounds
will you abandon before the start
for a comfortable roof of sadness?
or you will let the blood flow
for a humble tile of happiness?

You have to run to find the way out
but not on a stuck flat treadmill
the sweat will be almost the same
but you will never reach the door

Better believe in a dream
which will never come true

Who can select you?   *(Refrain)*
Who can eject you?
Who can neglect you?
Who can discriminate you?
Who can humiliate you?
when the scars in your look
bravely declare
your willingness to fight
Rejection doesn't exist
is just a boost to insist

The filings, misruled, are waiting
the magnet to give them direction
will or orders the only two choices
those with the positive magnitude
acquire the great mission to heal
and the easy adapts the negative
but has a deadline to be healed

The handicapped consciousness
is destined to sit in a wheelchair
can't move on the stairs but in line
the hands get dirty before a mile

Better believe in the greatest vision
which seems impossible to actualize

Who can select you?   *(Refrain)*
Who can eject you?
Who can neglect you?
Who can discriminate you?
Who can humiliate you?
when the scars in your look
bravely declare
your willingness to fight
Rejection doesn't exist
is just a boost to insist

The teddy bears in the line
play the drums with the same rhythm
do you want to be one of them?
just to be easily accepted
when the battery soon will be empty

Any exchange confirms defeat
Give without transactions
otherwise one day
you will be asked to give
what you will never have

Wear the colors of war
to live in peace
Don't wait for the chicken
to fly in your mouth
search for it tirelessly
while the saucepan is still full
don't waste your time
with the spices of an unknown truth

Doesn't exist promises
but gestures
Doesn't exist no
but open doors
Doesn't exist yeses
but closed sources
Doesn't exist small or protective lies
but growing problems which will never expire

Who can select you? *(Refrain)*
Who can eject you?
Who can neglect you?
Who can discriminate you?
Who can humiliate you?
when the scars in your look
bravely declare
your willingness to fight
Rejection doesn't exist
is just a boost to insist

We all fell in love   *(unavoidable passion)*
dived into the lust of passion
but who faced the war of the emotions
sourced from the true nature of a woman, not a name
on the verge of the ultimate feelings of pure instincts
an unavoidable attraction for both from a common secret
when the look struggles hard to flee
because it can't afford to see her beauty
and her steps are running further and further
because she desperately wants to turn back, not to suffer
Who cares what is going to happen in the end
when such strong qualitative foundations
are been structurally constructed
from within

Try to fly away
because I am not ready
try to forget me
because I will always
love you

Ground Zero

Compromise is a prison with an open door
the bars with fresh colors of green and blue
please hold them before the paint gets dry
never think that they are the grass and the sky

Even if you have a fast or slow car
or just a bicycle
you have to walk
in the desert, in the valley, on the road

Hope to be barefoot
pain to be the opportunity
easier to change your way

You shouldn't worry at all   *(Refrain)*
just wear a bulletproof passion
The fear of the unknown
is the fog of the distance
till the ground zero
to light the direction,
a tailor of your own map
always worth it to follow

Dilemma is a prison with an open door
the walls are painted with white or black
see the grey even if you are the only one
don't handcuff yourself to have company

Even if you have many or few shoes
or just a pair
you have to walk
in the rain, in the sunshine, on the snow

Hope not to be supported
loneliness not to feel alone
easier to find your own road

You shouldn't worry at all *(Refrain)*
just wear a bulletproof passion
The fear of the unknown
is the fog of the distance
till the ground zero
to light the direction,
a tailor of your own map
always worth it to follow

From human nature to biology
true pleasures lose their meaning
the infinity of the senses vanishes
in the body without spirit
becomes flesh without lust
but addictions to imagine
that it is still alive
wasting quality time
through automatic reactions
and is trying the impossible
to be loved
but even then gains the hope
in front of the mirror of Botox
the traitor to be betrayed

Why do you want to pretend
that you are someone else
by sacrificing your soul
just to lose yourself?
when
no one is more intelligent than you
for your plan
no one is more capable than you
for your mission
no one is wealthier than you
for your chamber
no one has a better appearance than you
for your partner
no one is more lucky than you
for your happiness
the only target
Do you care for something more?

No one can invest more time
for the things you care about
than you
to know them better
to own them more
to desire them more
to love them more

Don't overestimate the life
you can't live
because you are stuck with a dream
Don't underestimate the truth
because you can lie
to think that you are alive
when no one lives for ever

Be itchy in a stranger's memory
than in a queue of avoidance
by giving the best of you
to create a fresh new drop
to pour as another one
extract in a common bottle
to quench the thirst of the world
starting from your very own

You shouldn't worry at all *(Refrain)*
just wear a bulletproof passion
The fear of the unknown
is the fog of the distance
till the ground zero
to light the direction,
a tailor of your own map
always worth it to follow

We are still here!

Without Verdict

The trust oppressed in papers, not to count
no one believes the big, to stay in the small
not to see the forests, but their own trees
I don't like this world
What should I confess?

In shop windows the new trends
to be bought with unwilling deals
for a show in the neighborhoods
I don't care for this world
What should I confess?

Are you obliged with just a pair of shoes?
Or you are fighting for a bigger wardrobe?
But did you create something new?
for our world
What makes you think that you deserve more?

Everything or nothing   *(Refrain)*
for the right thing,
is an insane idea only
for an indecent world,
but a decision capable to break
the disoriented chain
Nothing to be the same
Without verdict
accused without accusation
for fifteen seconds of confession

Friendship is based on temporary materials
Love forgets to feel, is thrilled for the visible
Fragile is noticed only on the sent packages
I don't accept this world
What should I confess?

Pioneers were burned in the fire
the alternative never to prosper
masses to move in a box as free
I don't want this world
What should I confess?

Are you grateful with just a plate of soup?
Or do you want to have lucrative buffets?
But did you offer something unique?
for our world
What gives you the certainty that you deserve more?

Everything or nothing   *(Refrain)*
for the right thing,
is an insane idea only
for an indecent world,
but a decision capable to break
the disoriented chain
Nothing to be the same
Without verdict
accused without accusation
for fifteen seconds of confession

How many things do you have
but you never cared to have?
How many things don't you have
but you always cared to have?
How many times did you want to leave
but you had to stay?
How many times did you want to stay

but you had to leave?
and even then, how many times did you pray
this stagnation to remain?
The fear for the worst
ends the possibility for the best
to blindfold the wishes
the victims to be in the role of victimizers
to criticize those who dared to live
just to ban any determination
in a crowded isolation

Be tougher from within
not to accept the unacceptable
Be judgmental
in your own court
even if
you never ate an extra bite, because one is starving
even if
you never killed an insect, because you can't create life
even if
you never celebrate, because the kids play with slingshots
even if
you see all strangers as brothers
even if
you have put a glass brick in the world's transparent wall

We all are a part of this world
with bigger or smaller stakes
and every fairness
is depending on us
But you can't be fair
not even to yourself
when you care
only for your own good
a search in the abyss for rights
impossible to find
unnecessary to be activated

Patience is not a duty
you have to fight
for the moral beauty
be there
no matter what
with prosperity or hunger
with happiness or sorrow
with pleasure or pain
till you can't afford it any more
and then you will be able to gain
your fifteen seconds of confession

Everything or nothing   *(Refrain)*
for the right thing,
is an insane idea only
for an indecent world,
but a decision capable to break
the disoriented chain
Nothing to be the same
Without verdict
accused without accusation
for fifteen seconds of confession

The stars are exacting
even to appear on a flag
always must be proved
before any announcement

True leaders did
millions of steps
asking you for one

The Mirror of Yesterdays

For anyone, life lets always one crack open
at least one sunray to be able to interfere
but is comfortable even the poorest known
to need courage to push further the door

All mistakes of the past must be put in a sack
their heavy weight to be carried on the back
experiences not in a memory but on the sight
not to hunt your tail for the rest of your life

When the same and the same wins
the sense of smell can be used to it
to make the garbage like the grass
to be odorless

Be influenced from nothing *(Refrain)*
be inspired from everything
The mirror of yesterdays
is following your shadow
waiting for the wrinkle of wisdom
just one
as a signature to confirm
our brighter future

The muscles of the mind must be worked out
to grab and turn the clock's minute hand back
in insecurity always to be late without answers
the unnecessary to become necessary at once

Only the authentic pillars are self-luminous
the dependent power is impelled to an end
closed in a drawer with memory full of facts
glass legs to be broken for politics to adapt

When the hands fondle the ego
mating thinks that makes love
and the handshakes get colder
just for a hope

Be influenced from nothing   *(Refrain)*
be inspired from everything
The mirror of yesterdays
is following your shadow
waiting for the wrinkle of wisdom
just one
as a signature to confirm
our brighter future

It's not enough
to throw objects under the bridges
It's not enough
to blow candles once every year
It's not enough
to wait for comets to fall
It's not enough
to wish without wishes

We all have a charisma
not taller than our ceiling
but needs
soul-searching to find it
self-confidence to believe in it
a quest to bring it in to light
great efforts to live it

You must be ignored
to know what love is
You must be sad
to know what happiness is
You must be desperate
to know what opportunity is
You must be defeated
to know what victory is

Be influenced from nothing   *(Refrain)*
be inspired from everything
The mirror of yesterdays
is following your shadow
waiting for the wrinkle of wisdom
just one
as a signature to confirm
our brighter future

Love and war   *(unavoidable passion)*
in the same bottle
the beautiful gets provocative
in indirect directions
is lying to find the truth
to be protected
from the bigger muscles
attracted from an unknown mystery
chained from a useful secret
both seduced to discover
new dimensions of strength
to gain the mission to continue
what yesterdays left unfinished

Unavoidable Passion

We are both born in the unfair, to make it fair
because we are the two extreme survivors
in the conflict of our two different interests
is our first training to create a better world

The equality in two different shapes of qualities
enforces us to ascend on the pyramid of ourselves
punished from the undisputed invisible power
in the necessary process to change us for ever

I am not
who I was
because I felt you

The words can't speak *(Refrain)*
when the touch
insists
the flesh to be the mouthpiece
of our spirits
while two temples
are worshiping
one soul

Just our natural attraction can't build uniqueness
must be fed from the thirst of our insatiable senses
inside the limitless details appears our glass of water
not the time to be lost in the addictions of a habit

The simple level of intercourse can't create adults
just changes the rules of the games they used to
The passion must break the cellules into pieces
and each one to feel the expressions of the lust

You are not
who you were
because I touched you

The words can't speak   *(Refrain)*
when the touch
insists
the flesh to be the mouthpiece
of our spirits
while two temples
are worshiping
one soul

The two extreme opposites
start as females and males
and they have to cross over
their basic biological needs
to find their real identity
to be introduced as women and men
defined from their determination
to achieve their wishes
their life to have a purpose
where the physical pleasure
will start searching
for a more intense word
till it can't find any

Her sight higher
than her bare heels
rarely can pose it
to transform the desire

of the unavoidable passion
into love
her velvet body
is the house
to bring the refugee
who is searching for shelters
home
because the picture
needs pixels
the color
shading-off tints

No question
needs an answer
when your freedom
must be mine
without any compromise

Love and war
in the same bottle
the beautiful gets provocative
in indirect directions
is lying to find the truth
to be protected
from the bigger muscles
attracted from an unknown mystery
chained from a useful secret
both seduced to discover
new dimensions of strength
to gain the mission to continue
what yesterdays left unfinished

Her hair is hiding the face
but not the beauty
not the eyes to betray the thoughts
while she is waiting for the hand
to comfort them behind her ear
to unleash the core of the feelings
for the ceremony of the fateful acceptance
where the vows shouldn't be forgotten
an initiation for just the one
which is aiming to expand
for all the rest

The words can't speak   *(Refrain)*
when the touch
insists
the flesh to be the mouthpiece
of our spirits
while two temples
are worshiping
one soul

We all fell in love
dived in the lust of passion
but who faced the war of the emotions
sourced from the true nature of a woman, not a name
on the verge of the ultimate feelings of pure instincts
an unavoidable attraction for both from a common secret
when the look struggles hard to flee
because it can't afford to see her beauty
and her steps are running further and further
because she desperately wants to turn back, not to suffer
Who cares what is going to happen in the end
when such strong qualitative foundations
are been structurally constructed
from within?

Try to fly away
because I am not ready
try to forget me
because I will always
love you

The Waves of Circumstances

You think that you are walking on open roads
but you are in a wavy granary higher than you
be vigilant not to take the huge risk not to risk
not to remain with the visibility of centimeters

The waves of the wind are always changing
the given compass, needs tools to be fixed
it doesn't matter which way you will choose
the wage of strong faith will not let you lose

Don't stay focused on the wrapper
but the content
Don't underestimate any path
to find your own

What is yours, is mine *(Refrain)*
What is mine, is yours
when we quench our thirst
with the same water
The only treasury is within us
values with worth
There are no belongings
in the words of trust

The sonic waves will come to your ears
from bells or imams, one call for the same
it depends only from your place of birth
a lack of common sense activates sirens

Without innovation, life is a stone on the water
can make fancy jumps with waves for a while
but must be rowed out, the gravity not to win
or needs legs and weight of a frog, not to sink

Don't see the smile behind a title
but the course
Don't underestimate anyone
to find yourself

What is yours, is mine *(Refrain)*
What is mine, is yours
when we quench our thirst
with the same water
The only treasury is within us
values with worth
There are no belongings
in the words of trust

The possessions of circumstances
have the same statistics
from noon till afternoon
are changing after a week
to commit the same mistake
yet again
some years later

Clashes between us and them
for the same pie
a hunt for a bigger bone
Uniforms with beggarly salaries
care only for the donors
not the source
in global complexities
without any evaluation
for the quality of leadership

are following every order
just to protect their own children
when they are burying
their entire future for ever
as well for all of the above

What prison is this?
to smile without laughing
to cry without tears
to see without watching
to hear without listening
to be without being
to pity without pity
to be Godless
just for dependent independence
to make proud a bunch of people
and be ashamed of yourself
in front of all the rest
because you didn't dare
just don't forget
to find time for new luggage
for the wonderful journey
admitted in admiration

The waves
of the cereals, the wind,
the sound, the water,
are reactions
as circumstances of actions
don't wait like a beggar
to dawning

What is yours, is mine *(Refrain)*
What is mine, is yours
when we quench our thirst
with the same water

The only treasury is within us
values with worth
There are no belongings
in the words of trust

Exchange any fortune,
any fame, any prize
for three more days of peace
any conflict to have a meaning

IN OUR WORLD

Chapter Three
Character: extensive

The Fusion of Reaction

Our world has crocodile tears
to make you cry for real
takes the child from the mother
to teach you the unconditional love

Our world throws you crumbs
not to let you put your bread upside down
bothers you with beggars
to wonder why you are not one

But the bridges connect both sides
because the rivers can't be stopped

Our world
yours and mine
forces you to react
because you don't care to act

In the fusion of reactions *(Refrain)*
many are suffering
for the others just to consider
to act
to be one step ahead
than two steps back
A miracle in a world
without coincidences

Our world proceeds with imperialism
to make you understand your weaknesses
requires your papers
not to think that you are any different

Our world presents the extreme luxury
to comprehend that you are the victim
doesn't show the big picture
as you are a part of it, you have to find out

But the windows are constructed with glass
the light of the powerful sun to break in free

The same world
of enemies and friends
enforces you to consume
because you ignore the authenticity to produce

In the fusion of reactions   *(Refrain)*
many are suffering
for the others just to consider
to act
to be one step ahead
than two steps back
A miracle in a world
without coincidences

Our world is based on the economy
because you care about money
Our world focuses on the debts
because you like the easy ways
Our world sees the mathematics
because you don't want to contribute
Our world sends you the bill
because you don't take responsibilities

Who to blame for the robbery?
the policemen or the thieves
Who to blame for the bribery?
the officials or the citizens
Who to blame for the poverty?
the refugees or the inhabitants
Who to blame for the slavery?
the bosses or the employees

Why the world tells you the truth
when its source is inside you
Why the world serves justice
when you have to deny the wrong
Why the world protects you
when you don't see strangers as friends
Why the world accepts your uniqueness
when you don't care to improvise
When our only job
is to create a better world

But we walked on the moon
The black and white of the big boxes
took colors even in pocket devices
We put a hundred horses in small engines
We extended our feet to travel globally
But the eyes dazzle from the shiny
that's why some hospitals still
have human names
not from inventors but the "donors"
to confirm corruption
by taking merciless advantages
because the traffic jams make space
for the ambulances to pass

In the fusion of reactions *(Refrain)*
many are suffering
for the others just to consider
to act
to be one step ahead
than two steps back
A miracle in a world
without coincidences

Our world puts us in different entrenched camps
to sing different verses
but for the same problems
to make us understand
that we are brothers

The fusion of reaction
is been triggered
from a loan we all took
and quite a few enjoyed
but must be paid off
because our world
wants from us
more

The Standing Man

Life gave me a spirit and chained my legs
to throw me in the middle of the ocean
To survive

Should have been wealth in every corner
but is just projections of happiness
pills for sadness
shields for madness

Life gave me the tools to fight for justice
and put me in a rotten society as captive
To stand stronger

What more to demand
after such great honor
before the end

Surrendered defenses   *(Refrain)*
Offensive offenses
To score more than you will get
not to be a pawn
but a determining factor
the voice in empty ears
to know that you can stand
You, the standing man

Life gave me the power to be weaker than the weak
knowledge and faith to be stronger than the strong
To remember

Should have been equal all mankind
but is just professions with pairs of scales
loyalty behind bars
courtesy inside numbers

Life gave me everything I got, to be who I am
and took everything from me, not to forget it
To create more

Drop by drop in the bottle
of active patience
until it's full

Surrendered defenses   *(Refrain)*
Offensive offenses
To score more than you will get
not to be a pawn
but a determining factor
the voice in empty ears
to know that you can stand
You, the standing man

Why should I want power
when I cannot help the weak?
Why should I want fortune
when I cannot fulfill a common wish?
Why should I want fame
when I cannot stand the indecency?
Why should I want substitutes
when the adulterated honey can't be tastier?

Fraud can give you a thousand hectares
but is incapable to feed even your soul
when the spirits are empty
the hunger can't be defeated
and it will come after you
sooner or later
But when honesty earns only one
everyone will do the same
and prosperity will expand for ever
because of the unknown you
the standing man

Surrendered defenses *(Refrain)*
Offensive offenses
To score more than you will get
not to be a pawn
but a determining factor
the voice in empty ears
to know that you can stand
You, the standing man

The ifs, can't be considered
just confirm the lack of knowledge
of what life really is
takes time and faith
to know who you are
only through difficult pathways
you can find the main road
where nostalgia will not need to remember
because every next moment will be greater
capable of serving your heart
to be present where matters
not to smile when you must
nothing to be enough
to be the standing man

For every woman
to find the motive
to appreciate her existence
as the only way to be unleashed
her indescribable true beauty

For every society
to dare without fear
committed to live free

Because of you
The standing man

Surrendered defenses *(Refrain)*
Offensive offenses
To score more than you will get
not to be a pawn
but a determining factor
the voice in empty ears
to know that you can stand
You, the standing man

If I stand alone
I will be without a name
without home
without country
but if we stand together
we will abolish
the modern slavery
for good

You have to realize
that you are a prisoner
in a prison with an open door
to earn the willingness to escape

Our victory is to fight
any outcome is in God's hands
and we have to bend
in front of His greatness
no matter what
even if He wants from us
to stand
with the heads up

The Deadline

It's not a profession to collect money
with occupations you don't enjoy
and looking at your watch for the break
but a hobby which will let you one day
to be at a loose end without knowing why

The published investments build paper-thin walls
when everyone knows, they can't buy a real brick
in restricted knowledge the deposits bogged down
insecure from the lack to see new opportunities

How many rents
can buy your visibility?
How many days of vacations
can pay your loyalty?

Since when   *(Refrain)*
bribery named job
Since when
promises can be broken
Since when
love wants to see
Since when
friendship thinks the future
The clock is ticking
the deadline will expire

To have the same schedule day in and day out
to forget your needs for those of your children
it's a great sacrifice, which takes too courage
but doesn't count, because it is just an excuse
You can't educate them to dare, when you didn't

Smarter minds take advantage of your patience
and put idiots in luxury golden cells of hypocrisy
to make fun of your fatigue and make you wonder
in case you decide that this world has to change

Which science can stop
your will?
Which cause can breathe
without a purpose?

Since when   *(Refrain)*
bribery named job
Since when
promises can be broken
Since when
love wants to see
Since when
friendship thinks the future
The clock is ticking
the deadline will expire

The squares will be always crowded
for the fireworks
The calendars will always have numbers
to point the date
The teams will always win
at least one match
The news will always show projections
for some good indicators

To make you believe
that you can last
without duration

When you don't collect
simple stones
to exchange them
with worthier goods
because they are everywhere
why with ordinary thoughts
are you asking for more?
just because you are accepted
from societies which commit
the exact same mistake
where is not a certainty
that the easy money
can buy only
illusions

All the elements in life
diminish till they vanish
when you don't use them
or increase when you do
A sharp balance between
the kindest intentions
and monstrosities
like the weight-bars in the gym
higher than previous times
among good, bad
or nothing

Since when   *(Refrain)*
bribery named job
Since when
promises can be broken
Since when

love wants to see
Since when
friendship thinks the future
The clock is ticking
the deadline will expire

The dialogue must start
from yourself and then
your family, your friends,
your colleagues, your society,
your neighborhood, your city,
your country, your continent
To change the world
by changing you

The multilevel communication
must initiate today
because tomorrow
will be late

The Unexpected

The wind took the plume of a goose
because it wanted to continue flying
used to see higher, as part of a wing
plunged into the ink to write history
because it wants to be something more

You shouldn't beg for a job
because you are the job
be priceless in any domain you really love
to get more than you need before asking

Did your first step know
that you will run?
Did your first word know
that you will speak?

The unsuspected expected   *(Refrain)*
brings misery
in discount shop baskets
To suspect the unexpected
creates the phenomenon
we never knew
that we will enjoy it
so much

The pebble trundles on the coast
because it wants to leave its trace
used to take an aim on a target
and waits to jump on the water
because it cares to see another world

The suit can't make you prouder
exchange any undeserved title
with even a piece of wood you sculptured
the future to have a reason to protect you

Did your first letter know
that you will write essays?
Did your first spadeful on the beach know
that you will make mountains on the sand?

The unsuspected expected *(Refrain)*
brings misery
in discount shop baskets
To suspect the unexpected
creates the phenomenon
we never knew
that we will enjoy it
so much

Even a small gap
inside the leaden sky
is enough
to let the sunshine enters
to invade the sadness
and change the dull landscape
but do you expect that?

With the first drops
on your forehead
you run to find a shelter
if you are not from Ethiopia
One time stay
to face a problem deep in the eyes
and solve it from its roots
through the different gravity
of the same, but soaked clothes

the need of the umbrella
an item which wasn't always expected
but someone constructed it to protect you
as so many other things and knowledge
to make you work for the unexpected
by describing a new unknown
in our interactive continuity
to avail as you are availed

We all have different shape and capacities
to achieve our own unexpected
to fulfill our role in this world
all fingers are not the same
and open in the palm
point different directions
but must be gathered in a fist
to obtain power
otherwise
we will make ourselves at home
when we are runaways

When the first thought
thinks the negative
confirms stupidity
because inside everything
exists the positive
and when you see it
increases your intelligence
which makes you capable
to transform
the noise into sound
the wind into a tornado
the snowflake into an avalanche
the wish into life

The unsuspected expected   *(Refrain)*
brings misery
in discount shop baskets
To suspect the unexpected
creates the phenomenon
we never knew
that we will enjoy it
so much

The fire of the candle
will always flicker
in the darkness
but can be seen from far
to be rescued and saved
only if you have worked
for the unexpected
beyond the ordinary

Suspect the unexpected
every aspect of it
builds the lifetime

The Preconditions

What is essential in life has a heavy price
to make even your eyes flee from it
and pay heavier by being far, to return
with maturity and this time with faith

It's not a triumph to gain many fields
but to feed as many as possible
by keeping only the last plate for you
not to be insecure

When it's easier to walk
you have to run
When it's easier to run
you have to walk
To avoid unproductive habits

You always knew   *(Refrain)*
what the right thing was to do
and you punish yourself
to make you suffer
because inwardly
you are feeling
that you can offer
more

The true real work is always productive
progresses you by growing a knowledge
even in the most common services adds
strokes of brush to ensure our continuity

To achieve respect is not a noble target
can't be gained from thousands immoral
but even only one honest man is enough
to make it count

When it's easier to find the elevator
you have to find the stairs
When it's easier to find the stairs
you have to find the elevator
To avoid undesired compromises

You always knew *(Refrain)*
what the right thing was to do
and you punish yourself
to make you suffer
because inwardly
you are feeling
that you can offer
more

You must use your advantages
to increase them
not to lose them
like to think
not to lose your intelligence
like to act
not to lose your talents
like to create
not to lose your energy
like to produce
not to lose your integrity
like to love
not to lose your emotions
like to improvise
not to lose your personality
like to imagine

not to lose your faith
like to dare
not to lose your courage
as so many other elements
capable of preserving liberty
and without them
even if you have a big fortune
even if you are an icon for millions
you will be empty

You can be rich without money
but if you are ruled from numbers
you must accept their judgment
and as it is an unproductive case
they will wear lampblack
to find you in the darkness
to take the smile with which
you welcomed them

You can't serve two Gods
when there exists only One
in a world which shows the outside
because it's the outcome of the inside

The only thing that
no one else can imprison
but you
is your mind
can travel anywhere in any time
if you let it
imagination is a vital spice
to keep a vision alive
to hope is useless
actions bring results

If your body is been sold
and you don't accept it
doesn't exist slavery
and the slave-trade
will not endure

You always knew *(Refrain)*
what the right thing was to do
and you punish yourself
to make you suffer
because inwardly
you are feeling
that you can offer
more

Understand the truth
before any judgment
and if you decide never to lie again
you shouldn't worry
only few will continue to question you
because the rest will not afford
the answers

Capital

Money doesn't exist, it's just a
unit of measurement like the volt
indicates the popularity of the visible
and shows how much responsibility
you can carry or you want to avoid

How priceless is your house
when everybody gets it with compromises?
How priceless are your assets
when no one can explain their existence?

What if
capital is the truth?
What if
capital is the honesty?
People would have never cheated

How much costs a source?
valid for how long?
when the real one
is inside you

The capital defines   *(Refrain)*
the center of interest
and we point
where it will be
in minerals, in papers
or in the spirit
Became a tough choice
when it shouldn't

Monopoly is for the children
but adults play the same game
by thinking that it is for real
when to control a currency you must
support or enrich precocious creativity

How priceless are the banknotes
when everybody gets them from bribery?
How priceless is democracy
when we live in a period of corruption?

What if
capital is the intelligence?
What if
capital is the integrity?
People would have never been cheated

How much costs a follower?
gets paid to admire
when to count for real
must find his own way

The capital defines   *(Refrain)*
the center of interest
and we point
where it will be
in minerals, in papers
or in the spirit
Became a tough choice
when it shouldn't

The rich have access to money
to lose everything they've got
through the process of greed
of their blindfolded ignorance
sourced from
their subconscious need
to be protagonists in soap operas

We all are in a movie
of a silent assassination
where the absence of coins
makes death a possibility
in a wrongdoing system
incomprehensible as capitalism
where even protests wait
a banknote behind the back
to yell against it
and vast majorities get dizzy
in a pantomime of a need

What would have been capital?
if we had been lacking
of food, or water, or oxygen
or perishing from diseases
Seems that it is been defined
from necessities
but the ideas beg desperately
the charities of thunder
when without new ideas
we can't survive

If a tsunami is about
to erase a city from the map
and only few can confront it
how much should they ask
to save lives?

The producers of tomorrow's capital
can't be understood from stagnation
are renamed as public enemies
when the micro-politics return
in the fight of illusions
for the madness to gain
what capital used to be yesterday
not even today

If you are getting happy
by stealing from others
you just make fun of yourself
we all live inside the same
self-destructive system
which doesn't have a name
but is eaten from within
and the only question is
who will be the first
and who the last

The capital defines *(Refrain)*
the center of interest
and we point where it will be
in minerals, in papers
or in the spirit
Became a tough choice
when it shouldn't

How priceless is your existence
when your steps don't enrich our future?
How priceless are your rights
when you misjudge your own comforts?
How priceless are your thoughts
when they are making no difference?
How priceless is your opinion
when you can't afford to say the truth?

Capital is something
that money can't buy
but must be acquired
in an ownership which can't be lost

Don't beg for mercy from merciless eyes
when you compromise
you're worth nothing
when you don't
you are priceless
because
you are the capital

Faith of Attraction

We live in a world of magnets
beauty between courage and consumption
to magnetize the magnitude of you

What attracts us
has no shape
has no name
has no questions
at the start
but has a purpose
to make us feel alive

A thought, an idea, a vision
of faithful actions
make me
never to remember pain

What took you so long? *(Refrain)*
The entire world in your body
Move forward
in the magnetic fields of will
without denying logic
without denying passion
both are belongings
of the faith of attraction

We live in a world of equations
maturity between zero and infinity
to find today the vastness of tomorrow

What distracts us
has shape
has name
has questions
at the start
with the purpose
the temporary to be permanent

A look, an existence, a touch
of a sculptured soul
makes me
never to forget you

What took you so long?   *(Refrain)*
The entire world in your body
Move forward
in the magnetic fields of will
without denying logic
without denying passion
both are belongings
of the faith of attraction

From what you saw
from what you missed
from what you heard
from what you learned
from what you won
from what you lost
from what you felt
from what you ignored
from what you did
and from what you didn't
sourced even your touch

The numbers
attract the body
the beauty
attracts the heart
the faith
attracts the mind
to find the way for the soul
to become spirit

What took you *(Refrain 2)*
so long?
the entire world
in your body

Money is just the motive
it's like a Brazilian carnival
ostentatious and crowded
but the joy doesn't last for long
to make the world tougher
to compel you to grow up
and finally to find a real purpose
from the dark narrow back alleys
to make you search for one thing
and one thing only
the light

Heroes live in pain
they don't care about themselves
but for the common interests
your kindness makes them exist
your fears make them suffer
because you have to be unleashed
the warmth of comforts
doesn't last for long
but entraps you in the stagnation
to preserve the stability you got used to

and makes your efforts
forget having passion
when to be where you please
you don't need to ask questions

What took you so long? *(Refrain)*
The entire world in your body
Move forward
in the magnetic fields of will
without denying logic
without denying passion
both are belongings
of the faith of attraction

When you will find
your faith of attraction
you must bend your head
in front of its wisdom
with the eyes down
to show trust
and submission
not just respect

First the soul goes out
and then faith
which means
that if you are not
ready to die
for what you believe in
you never lived

Useful Fear

Austerity is the brakes of the vehicle
which lost direction on a steep descent
and the passengers fight for the steering wheel
before experiencing the crash of their lifetime

The law-abiding don't know many laws
and when one of them goes against logic
needs a fight with all powers to be changed
because to function must serve humanity

Fear the decision
to be one of them
because you are one of us

Every step back   *(Refrain)*
loses
a step ahead
Fear to surrender
unafraid to be on the trip
of unorthodox sacrifices
to find
your freedom

The debt creates big craggy mountains
to make it more difficult for you to climb
to empty your pockets to be flexible and
competent for the new higher standards

The bills are eating your moments
to make you decide if slavery will continue
but the comfort to pay them lets you forget
from where you found that possibility

Fear the wish
to be forgotten
because you left nothing behind

Every step back   *(Refrain)*
loses
a step ahead
Fear to surrender
unafraid to be on the trip
of unorthodox sacrifices
to find
your freedom

Fear to feel ingratitude
even for the tiniest forms of life
The ladybug predicts
the heavy winters
months before coming
and by trying to find a shelter
is entering also your home
to inform you that earth is a living organism
that nature wants to protect you
and to create in you the fear to throw
litter on the soil or water
because seven billion people
will do the same
and you will discover
the minimum consequences
on the few weeks of your vacations
by being in inhospitable places

The cities have pigeons
because they have the most sensitive legs
a sensor for an earthquake before coming
and to teach you
to be vigilant when everything is calm
to become proactive before problems arrive
because doesn't exist
a system to preserve prosperity
we have to progress through changes
we must be better than yesterday

Be prepared for the worst
and hope for the best
be like the beetle
which can carry ten times its weight
but do it with unselfish hands
to fear to return back
not to be who you were
but who you always wanted to be
because your real idol is the better you
Tomorrow is …
another day

When the power is based on the codes of contacts
and not on the uniqueness of actions
no matter how many square meters it provides
it makes you live in a small boat without doors
which turns to the side of your every step
and when you finally sit in the middle
the waves will come to find you
to remind you that you need foundations
to stabilize and prosper
and without them
you have to pray to be on a lake
but if you are on the ocean
better hope to be

near a peninsula of an enemy
than to be exposed
to the law of the fishes

Every step back   *(Refrain)*
loses
a step ahead
Fear to surrender
unafraid to be on the trip
of unorthodox sacrifices
to find
your freedom

The believed civilization
is on the wings of a mosquito
thrilled to find a swamp
to make its eggs
and drinks blood
to survive one more day
a process to make it forget
that it will be eaten
from the birds
to continue to warble

Unseen Mercenaries

Any job or occupation just for the money
is not a work but a bribery, just to support
a system which doesn't care about anyone
and when you find it out, it will be too late

Criminals behind the façade of legitimate professions
are connected with a network based on virtual needs
and they are ready to gag or kill the consciousness of truth
because if it prevails, they will lose what they never owned

The briber
has a philosophy
because many recipients exist
but if you don't have a different one
you will be a marionette

The body *(Refrain)*
without a soul
smells
with a soul in a coma
rules
but when the main source of energy
doesn't function
how far can you go?

The borrowed liquidity creates invisible cells
for armies which have accepted their modern slavery
but they can't see it, by watching the traditional one
and they hope that changes will come by doing nothing

The diplomas are the first stair out of a thousand
but even these few centimeters of a higher view
make the people squeeze papers for profits
when the essential juices of their time vaporize

The assassin
has an ideology
because he's just doing his job
but if you don't have a different one
you will be a victim

The body   *(Refrain)*
without a soul
smells
with a soul in a coma
rules
but when the main source of energy
doesn't function
how far can you go?

Whatever is sourced from volition
has foundations
but anything based on money
doesn't
is just a virtual reality
ready to be evaporated
from volatility

If you lose a banknote
nobody will know that it is yours
doesn't have your name on it
and it will never have it
makes no difference
if you gain more of them
except some idiots around you
trying to persuade you

that you have power
just for their own personal interests
but they are not enough to change reality

It is easier to pull the trigger
than to create a weapon
that's why you have to think it
over and over again
before unleashing the fire
because in our world
the bullets are the money
but need sophisticated establishments
to function
with the main purpose not to kill
but to teach

The politics offer publicity
for some to become the donors
with the money they will never have
to guide the needs of the pockets
in exchange to appear as lawmakers
for issues they never thought before
and make them suffer from gossips
because the given power costs
and by paying this price
they gain the immunity
not to be accused
for what really matters

In a world which blames
someone else for its failures
anonymity is a privilege
when no one knows you
you can't be a martyr

The body   (Refrain)
without a soul
smells
with a soul in a coma
rules
but when the main source of energy
doesn't function
how far can you go?

The only certain well-disposed mercenary
is within the brighter side of yourself
we don't live in a world of angels
unless if you start
suspecting the opposite
the invisible to become visible
by looking with the mind
not just with the eyes
through higher frequencies
you couldn't see before
to discover a brand-new world
where any sore trial doesn't harm
but heals

Premature

You can't see a miracle, if you don't know what it is
the sea will not cut in two, when you can learn to swim
Every day can be a new wonder or just nothing at all
it depends if a peaceful cup of coffee is an obvious factor

Everybody knows that the fruits on the trees will ripen
but who can even imagine if a simple thought will thrive
it depends totally on you, if an idea will become reality
cynicism will be always there to strengthen your faith

Don't expect
with your first words
to write history

Create *(Refrain 1)*
the smallest
the most humble
the most unknown
which maybe
seems silly
but create anything you care
to find everything you want

It is very difficult to find the way of your gut feeling
the delays will push it further, to integrate maturity
your road map is in the questions you never felt to ask
because their new answers need to be given from you

If you choose a position irrelevant and far from your will
the truth will be a wedge among your chair's abutments
and all the years that you try to hide it even from you
just measure the precious time that you have lost already

Don't expect
with your first plan
to make a fortune

Create *(Refrain 1)*
the smallest
the most humble
the most unknown
which maybe
seems silly
but create anything you care
to find everything you want

Contribute your uniqueness
and it doesn't matter
if it will seem practical or useless
if it will be for today or ten years after
if you will influence many or just one
because it will bring
the best side of yourself

We didn't know about lamps
when we were lighting candles
We didn't know about forks
when we were eating with the hands
We didn't know about tables
when we were sitting on the ground
We didn't know about houses
when we were living in caves
but a miracle happened
and no one wonders any more

Don't think
that the fight
will ever end
even if you are occupied
with something
you always wanted
or something
you never liked
don't expect
someday to win
or someday to lose
life goes on
and on and on

The entrenchments rarely brought
better and significant changes
that's why the successful sword
is not sharp or shiny
but full with rust
forgotten in the attic
which used to demonstrate
the sculptured scabbard
and the artistic letters
on the not-honed metallic blade
which were describing
words of bravery
for peaceful new beginnings

We all have a role
in this world
those who contribute
become the members
and those who care
only for themselves
become the victims
even if we like it or not

is the unavoidable process
to make us
stronger, smarter, wiser
for the necessary evolution
of the human species

Don't think *(Refrain 2)*
that the fight
will ever end
don't expect
someday to win
or someday to lose
life goes on
and on and on

In our world
even the words cost
make them count

The Idiosyncrasy of Whys

The main direction is in the unanswered questions
in a rough and long distance without confirmations
guidelight to step foot in the beginning of forever
where willingness will be obliged to serve the soul

Why you should ask
for something you feel
for something you know
for something you believe
for something which is natural to you
when no answer
can change your mind

Don't ask me why
the reasons lose identity
take your own oath

In a world of magnets *(Refrain 1)*
questions need no mouths
answers need no ears
visions need no predictions
future needs no past
The idiosyncrasy of whys
in a few parables

Philosophy is the speech of wisdom for everyday life
It is also the roads, the signposts and the traffic lights
to personalize your own ideology of independence
not to follow the profane, to think that you are alive

Why you shouldn't ask
for something alternative
for something unknown
for something unusual
for something which seems impossible
when with existing materials
we have built new foundations

Don't ask me why
the words lose their meaning
make your own reckoning

In a world of magnets *(Refrain 1)*
questions need no mouths
answers need no ears
visions need no predictions
future needs no past
The idiosyncrasy of whys
in a few parables

The secrets are hiding in the shadows *(Refrain 2)*
and waiting for the light to find them
No question
makes you breathe
No answer
makes you wiser
The reasons are profound

Why search for miracles
when the hammerhead sharks see better
Why wait for wonders
when you are taller than years ago
Why squeeze the obvious
when you are the new unknown
Why remain with the answers
you already know?

The knowledge can ask why
with the purpose to be wise
to be able to fill its warehouses
one day to feed new answers
because if wisdom decides to flee
from a city of millions
every neighborhood will become empty
choose to keep it
behind the high walls
to make them transparent
and if you feel
that you don't need it today
it is a certainty
that you will need it tomorrow

Ask yourself why
you feel comfortable
in the insecure securities
of the professions of permanency
which don't develop growth
in their unproductive attitudes
but make you oppose your brothers
to keep at least some parts of the stagnation visible
when your stocks and bonds will be manipulated
inflation will not pity your bank accounts
and nobody will ask you
to recapitalize the same failures
which have no mood
to change behavior

In our world
you have to choose
among two unavoidable ways
either to contribute
by defending justice
or to get victimized

by accepting the unacceptable
a course to make your heart
gigantic or microscopic
don't ask me why

The secrets are hiding in the shadows (Refrain 2)
and waiting for the light to find them
No question
makes you breathe
No answer
makes you wiser
The reasons are profound

In a world of magnets (Refrain 1)
questions need no mouths
answers need no ears
visions need no predictions
future needs no past
The idiosyncrasy of whys
in a few parables

Only on a blank cheque
can sign
the ink of trust
where priceless
can't be bothered from papers
where love
can't be forgotten
where friendship
offers both shoulders
to the broken legs
till they walk again

The Amortization of a Dream

Everything starts with the quest of a foolish believe
underlined the words of books, no one orders to read
messy written papers in places you never used to be
dim the colors of the flags under the same purpose

The daydreamers don't improvise, just complain
but actions of inspiration make dreams come true
are depicted as visions to define the real missions
to drink the essences of your life till the last drop

No revolution
was born
with a name

The scepters *(Refrain)*
don't make the kings
Success can't
include compromises
Be a visionary
your efforts to believe
one day the impossible
to be possible
the amortization of a dream
in a vision

The immune system is very strong without using medicines
sadness and stress are the worst enemies to make it weak
they are entering in popular carriers, far from main visions
and health rings a bell to take you out from a virtual world

Don't undermined the creative idea of who you are
to be in a field that you will never be good enough
and to become a legitimate thief, to buy more time
with the money that you will never manage to keep

No guilt
can be washed out
with water

The scepters   *(Refrain)*
don't make the kings
Success can't
include compromises
Be a visionary
your efforts to believe
one day the impossible
to be possible
the amortization of a dream
in a vision

Be a positive conductor of good
to receive the gifts
that belongs to you
to be able to make
the impossible
possible
to reach what seems unreachable
to see the eyes you missed
to be where you always wanted
not to be obligatory for you
to belong in a flock of sheep
where the shepherds are the wolves
and the lions which keep the balance
will not tolerate much longer
the wrongdoings to continue
but if you want to live with lies
you will be judged from them

Admit your fears
to strengthen yourself
the fear of truth
can finish in a moment
to redeem you
When you aren't afraid to see
you shouldn't be afraid to decide
when you aren't afraid to breathe
you shouldn't be afraid to be free
when you aren't afraid to wish
you shouldn't be afraid to act
when you aren't afraid to eat
you shouldn't be afraid to risk
are the same thing

Any choice
relevant or irrelevant
must have the same target
to be on the road of a vision
Is not enough
to be almost there
almost present
almost ready
How soon is almost?
It is not enough to go far
but further than you can
not be a champion
but a complete individual

Drink the bitterness
to lose the joy of moments
which are the siege of the ordinary
to deprive the essence of your life
You must throw your time
in front of your feet
to become experiences of stones

to build the bridge
from knowledge to wisdom
happiness to have duration

The scepters   *(Refrain)*
don't make the kings
Success can't
include compromises
Be a visionary
your efforts to believe
one day the impossible
to be possible
the amortization of a dream
in a vision

Be a visionary
the thoughts which can't be understandable
to be understood

The burnt laboratory
can be a fresh new start
the cynicism
can be the leverage
the poverty
can be the mean
Prioritize. Visualize. Actualize
Simultaneously, spontaneously, with transparency
Excuses have no place in real life
The amortization of your dreams
in the fulfillment of a vision
Not the breath
to be an obsession

Reciprocal

You are accused that you belong in the mob
in a category named as ordinary people
blindfolded, you follow the mainstream
and ask others to give you your rights

If you need to be recognized from a list
you will never afford justice to prevail
If your incomes are based on contacts
you won't accept transparency to thrive

What unites us
are the everlasting values
honor, integrity, trust
solidarity to have a meaning

Ethical and unethical   *(Refrain)*
the North and South Pole
the one you live it
and the other you imagine
but even if you wear gloves
the cold will remain
and someone will take them from you
Only the warmth
of our consciousness
can bring the equator

You are accused that you belong in a special group
don't sell yourself for smiles to open you the doors
you can be used to any luxury within some months
but it will take you a lifetime to find what's missing

If you have found easy ways in a micro-world
the stronger will never respect your existence
If you don't care about poverty and indignity
the tax invasion and debts will bring you there

What divides us
are the personal interests
greed, ingratitude, temptations
glory without foundations

Ethical and unethical *(Refrain)*
the North and South Pole
the one you live it
and the other you imagine
but even if you wear gloves
the cold will remain
and someone will take them from you
Only the warmth
of our consciousness
can bring the equator

The prayers
want to see your efforts
to know
that you don't make fun
with something that you shouldn't
when it's been given to you
all the tools you need
to fulfill your wishes

When everybody demands barters
what chances have peace?
what chances have prosperity?
what chances have love?
what chances have humanity?

The societies are isolating the heroes
because they irrigate any possible point
from where a dangerous spark can shoot out
international, national or domestic
but when the field is getting full with dry grass
the fire only can be postponed for later
the cleverness watches further than the nose
to make the difference in the meanwhile
when the slyness is the old-fashioned mask
to disguise unsuccessfully stupidity
where the egoism has the first role
and when it sees a handicapped man
feels sorry only for itself
because it's been exposed
in a disturbing image
That explains why your selfishness
can't offer anything for a better world
but is a great threat for yourself
because who will support you
when the time will come?

Don't use your children as a shield
for the things you didn't dare to do
you can't protect them
by taking them from school
but by erasing any wrong you notice
to offer them a bright future
not to bury it before it started

Every acceptance
of an undeserved dime
of any scale or level
is a declaration of war
because it will miss
from someone else's deficiency
You shouldn't forget
that the family of a dead solder
never stops to mourn
even if it was in the oath of his duty
in order to serve a county
of a world
in which
we all are responsible

Ethical and unethical *(Refrain)*
the North and South Pole
the one you live it
and the other you imagine
but even if you wear gloves
the cold will remain
and someone will take them from you
Only the warmth
of our consciousness
can bring the equator

If someone asks your help
as a politician
you will think that many more will come
as a humanitarian
you will be glad to offer whatever you can
but with which way
you want to be judged
as an entity or as a whole?

A profane world
is searching for rumors
when we really are
our actions

The Width of Impact

What are the chances of any army with millions
which doesn't know how to create even a spark
against few who has invented the rocket-science
orders of salaries can't cover your responsibilities

The trade unions allege that maintain gained privileges
but for how many days is the fresh-cooked food eatable?
only the uniqueness of each worker upgrades the rights
and qualitative work enforces the incomes to increase

Why be in a riot
when without your skills
shouldn't have been production?

What chances   *(Refrain 1)*
has the arrogance of nothing
blindfolded from empty digits
against
the intelligence of creation?

To create surplus values   *(Refrain 2)*
is the purpose of our lives
what you are
to be expanded
your identity
to be invented
the width of impact
to depend on you

A lot of fraternities are based on the humiliation of their members
to diminish till vanishes any possibility of no, in the course to follow
and no matter how many or how rich they are, they can't confront
not even one person who doesn't care to breathe without freedom

Even if you have found the way to transform stones into gold
it is not certain that you will thrive or anyone will ever know you
because you are not from gentlefolk with borrowed firewood
but only huge volumes of quality time can buy wisdom, not money

Why be in a clash
when without your opinion
shouldn't have been solutions?

What chances   *(Refrain 1)*
has the arrogance of nothing
blindfolded from empty digits
against
the intelligence of creation?

To create surplus values   *(Refrain 2)*
is the purpose of our lives
what you are
to be expanded
your identity
to be invented
the width of impact
to depend on you

When the interest rates
are almost the same
how the creditors
can be different
just bureaucracy offers jobs
to work without working
to think without thinking

to serve without servicing
to offer without offering
to control without controlling
to provide without providing
to defend without defending
to protect without protecting
to ask for your identity without identity
to make you believe
that you exist without existence
to achieve without achievements
to be recognized without recognition
by being efficient without efficiency
because it's easier to read a book
than to write your very own

There were never wars
between the rich and the poor
the generals were always watching
the battles with the binoculars
but between those who found a snug berth in a wrongdoing
and those who wanted to, but they couldn't manage to enter
an unnecessary fight from the one party to gain
the privileges from the other
determined to commit exactly the same mistakes
but the lack of serious ideology
fills the battlefields of decisions with corpses
fatalities without names
categorized for the kindness of hypocrisy
as collateral damage

Be the light
in periods of darkness
be the transparency
in countries of corruption
be the ethics
in cities of sin

be the love
in neighborhoods of hate
be the electricity
in the peaceful fields of stagnation
to find at least yourself

Be the peacemaker *(Refrain 3)*
in the conflicts of compromised interests
to fight even subconsciously
for the greater good
undistracted
from the problems of the moments
careless for the outcome
and The Almighty will ensure
no enemy to prevail
against you

What chances have the victims of semiotics
which are raped from the theatrical deception
against the restless lion-heart innovators
who are about to break their chains?

What chances have the ignorant dancing bodies
which never earn the luxuries they taste
against the consciously deserted warriors
who ate locusts to survive?

What chances have the mouths of cynicism
which must laugh loudly with silly jokes
against the marathons of walking monks
to be transmitted the truthful living?

What chances have the full stomachs of apathy
which are faking charities for a second dessert
against the army of true heroic volunteers
whose every bite they offer saves lives?

Takes a lifetime
to be prepared
for the things
which are about to come
not to be the weakest link any more
and you will never know
when something will happen
if you are right or wrong
but you will understand
that you can't defend yourself
without your dignity

What chances   *(Refrain 1)*
has the arrogance of nothing
blindfolded from empty digits
against
the intelligence of creation?

Be the peacemaker   *(Refrain 3)*
in the conflicts of compromised interests
to fight even subconsciously
for the greater good
undistracted
from the problems of the moments
careless for the outcome
and The Almighty will ensure
no enemy to prevail
against you

In our world
the choice is always
up to you

It doesn't matter
if the theories of conspiracy
are truthful or not
because their existence proves
that your opinion has gravity

Only the strong populations
with the amalgam of virtues
can build great nations
capable of choosing leaders with a vision
not to follow them
but altogether to be tuned
after a greater cause
to be created the womb of democracy

PART B

Divided Heroes
(Central Title)

Chapter Four
Character: preliminary

Divided Heroes

If you would have had a dream like mine
you would have never been a hero
but ripped, soaked, shreds of a sail
true hope of a raft on an angry wavy ocean

You would have been a tired thirsty castaway
careless to return in unproductive warm nests
sculpturing every day for better truthful means
a lone diver of wisdom, in a desolated isolation

Feel the sun and the rain
it is moving sand
to be blessed without a name

Dream like me *(Refrain)*
to dream like you
to fight together
for common perpetual values
All became heroes
behind emblems of the past
to unify as dreamers
for the milestones of tomorrow

If you would have had a dream like mine
you would have never been a hero
but with chained hands behind your back
without having for nothing to apologize

You would have been exiled as an enemy
by trying to prevent the worst during peace
the old cloths can't persuade anyone to listen
in a world which fakes changes through wars

Enjoy the moments you can
by carrying a candle
to feel at least safe for tonight

Dream like me *(Refrain)*
to dream like you
to fight together
for common perpetual values
All became heroes
behind emblems of the past
to unify as dreamers
for the milestones of tomorrow

Happiness is a transported light
is not an unburned fire
to feel a winner without a fight

Humanity is haunted
from the vastness of eternity
echo across the centuries
is building
brick by brick
hand in hand
till the last drop of blood
our future
and is waiting for the daylight
to bring a brand-new day

We don't become heroes
because we want
but because we must
unless if you prefer
to live in a world
which wishes
never to dawn

Pain wrote history
for the blindfolded ignorance to read
Tons of weights on the shoulders
but still the fingers found the strength to support the knees
Despair bent the heads for a moment
just for a tear to meet the soil
Hundred times have been crossed self limits
for the unknown paths of new beginnings

In one way or another
you have to choose
spiritual missiles or heavy truce
The destination is unknown
the gravity of leverage on your own
Divided heroes or unite
is just a settlement between the urgency
of a human right
Two voices in the minds of shame
unfairness or justice
are not the same
it depends which one
you want to blame

Without heroes
you would have never existed
Without you
we would have never resisted
Is there any reason for us to fight

between the darkness and solid light?
Be restless
till you truly find
what is next
for your state of mind

Dream like me   *(Refrain)*
to dream like you
to fight together
for common perpetual values
All became heroes
behind emblems of the past
to unify as dreamers
for the milestones of tomorrow

Be an unafraid witness
of your soul
like the tailored clouds
inside the sunset
of an endless horizon

The drums of war
are creating heroes
when they are silent
Sacrifice is not a choice
Glory is not a noise

Unchain Impossible

The mountain became a rock
Ordinary people deify the clock
The souls' bridges turns into walls
The great is gone, to stay the small

See the entire world around
Hear the minefield's sound
as peace looks like war
the darkness is confused more

Look at you
the boy you used to be
thirty years in a moment
you thought you can see

Boy to man *(Refrain)*
unchain impossible
you can't break the dreams
you can't break the promises
the molecules whisper
the vastness of possible
but who wants to hear
in a river of fear

Draw the painting with every yes
keep the best colors for the less
see maturity as tremendous duty
responsibility as perfect beauty

Sacrifice good days for more to come
to gain the chance for a better plan
with closed eyes it's difficult to win
strange game, holiness against sin

Recall the boy
you used to be
in an instant moment
to realize that you are not free

Boy to man   *(Refrain)*
unchain impossible
you can't break the dreams
you can't break the promises
the molecules whisper
the vastness of possible
but who wants to hear
in a river of fear

The voice of a boy
you barely remember
doesn't let you to sleep and surrender
But his wounds are on your skin
His footsteps haunt your screen
His losses preserve your pain
His winnings make you pray
His choices kept you alive in vain

Imagine a dialogue
with the picture
of the boy you used to be
thirty years instantly
in front of the mirror
you and him
Listen his voice

inside your mind
his questions are unstoppable
Did you conquer the world?
Did you become a rising star?
Did you reach the sky?
At least, did you learn how to fly?
Or you are still grounded
behind closed doors
inside a u-turn
without asking why, any more

Make a pledge
to gain back
his pure eyes
heart and soul
not to be deafened any more
from the sirens
of illusionary lusts
but the real ones
Tools you always had
as perfect weapons
never to surrender

It was a dream
to be fulfilled
must be unleashed
in life's front-line scene
to initiate the highest glory
every moment
to conquer the vanity
of the same boring story

Boy to man   (Refrain)
unchain impossible
you can't break the dreams
you can't break the promises
the molecules whisper
the vastness of possible
but who wants to hear
in a river of fear

Boy to man
unchain impossible
but to change any moment
is always possible

Screams of Silence

From kilometers with naked feet
till meters with shiny shoes for school
Witness
the patience for education

From a heavily loaded ant
till the orbit of a satellite
Witness
the inspiration for progress

Don't wait fruitless thoughts
don't confuse
miracles with magic
Harms time
wounds logic

The whole world is one body
thirsty to hear
your scream of silence
to mobilize justice

Be aware   *(Refrain)*
what defines you
Witness
the uniqueness of your existence
In the screams of silence
are the great efforts
every day to be
a new miracle

From the first step in the room
till the footsteps on the moon
Witness
our destiny to move forward

From a piece of sand
till a rocky mountain
Witness
the probability of growth

Don't wait imaginary thoughts
Don't confuse
strength with weakness
The lost time
injures reality

The entire world is one soul
is famished to hear
your scream of silence
to harmonize truth

Be aware *(Refrain)*
what defines you
Witness
the uniqueness of your existence
In the screams of silence
are the great efforts
every day to be
a new miracle

Listen
what the others have to say
See
with the eyes of your opponent
Forget
to bargain for a better sale

Ignore
the excuses for a harmless way

Wear
lenses to visualize eternity
Focus
on the true colors of life
Acknowledge
teasers for permanent prosperity
to preserve liberty
by surrendering the defenses of possible
to experience
the independence of impossible

Be aware *(Refrain)*
what defines you
Witness
the uniqueness of your existence
In the screams of silence
are the great efforts
every day to be
a new miracle

The tongues
prefer to be cut
than to admit
that they have nothing to say
but the woods of the forests
can't be transformed
into horses
what is meant to happen
will happen
no matter what
logic to be given

From the decrepit hut
till the most luxury palace
Witness
the urgency to breathe in wisdom

From falling in love
till the deepest beliefs
Witness
the liberation for emotions

From the mother
till the wild lioness
Witness
the instinct for protection

From the white clouds
till the leaden sky
Witness
the passion for light

Be aware   *(Refrain)*
what defines you
Witness
the uniqueness of your existence
In the screams of silence
are the great efforts
every day to be
a new miracle

The only revolution
is any creation
a scream of silence
silently is influencing
our perspective
to continue
Doesn't need answer

for any accusation
because defines our future
Every day to be
a brand-new miracle

Invisible Absence

The glamorous shoes without a trace of dust in the wardrobe
worked as plastic boots to be able to walk inside the thick mud
the depth deepens and the knees can't support enough any more
but they don't know why
because of the invisible absences

The head bends to find the keys and unlock the rewarded emptiness
the whole virtual profane world behind the closed unviable secure door
the crystal chandelier with the fancy lights not for long necessary
velvet and silk numbed the body
not to get electrified with a thought

The invisible absences packaged a golden cell
the enthusiasm soon forgotten
just the clenched hands holding the cold metal bars
has remained
shadowing the naked life, exposed in the hardest winter

Papers from the past *(Refrain)*
bought the time
a torch as the guidelight
for the darkest pathways
Invisible absence
a vaccine for uncertainty
but can't hide for long
the empty soul

The expensive masks full of dust untouched in the big wardrobe
the tight-stretched trained metal skin doesn't need them any more
takes automatically the necessary forms for any circumstance
and the mirror doesn't know why
because of the invisible absence

In the spacious luxury room with the heavy wooden bed
perfectly proportioned figures smoothly swayed to undress
but the pulses don't open any more the pupils of the eyes
the emotions are tied in the pocket
to express faithless pleasures

The invisible absence packaged a golden cell
the music soon silenced
just the pushed face among the cold metal bars
has remained
shadowing the homeless beggar on the bench

Papers from the past   *(Refrain)*
bought the time
a torch as the guidelight
for the darkest pathways
Invisible absence
a vaccine for uncertainty
but can't hide for long
the empty soul

The invisible absence
doesn't let you see
the true despair
blinds the eyes
between everything and nothing
without giving you the right
to share

The cell is only in the mind
is just a prison door
without any barriers around
Just make a side step
few centimeters separate you
from a lifetime
to notice the forest
and not just the leaf
In the visible presence
is the deepest belief

There is no love without pain
There is no redemption without spirit
There is no absence without knowing the presence
There is no I exists only we

Papers from the past *(Refrain)*
bought the time
a torch as the guidelight
for the darkest pathways
Invisible absence
a vaccine for uncertainty
but can't hide for long
the empty soul

Unfathomed Traces

Youth's magnets held her fingers inside yours, on the coast
but the feelings didn't last for long

Alone you felt the harmony of the refreshing water
but your footsteps are gone

You cared your sign to remain even from the biggest wave
but the tide took your new trace away

The biggest mirror of the sky is carrying the wisdom of the centuries
You were too young to know

The nearest mountain gave you the choice for a new promise
You were old enough to start

You started to run on it and the passion covered you with sweat
not to feel defeated again

In the middle of the way you got tired, the ascent increased
a dilemma initiated your new life

Signs of life, unchallenged light
Unfathomed traces
the mercenaries of your visions
Be prepared to lose everything without regret
You have no other belongings except your self

The hardest battle   *(Refrain)*
against any enemy
but between you and you
the longest distance
Unfathomed traces the aid
for your hopeless hope
The greatest view
an invitation for the top

Don't abandon, your wings are not strong enough
to let you fly away

The knowledge of the centuries is the sharpest rock
when you are approaching the top

there the titans with bleeding muscled shoulders from the rope
to move the earth to help your hope

Your choices can betray you, can momentarily humiliate you
your innocence can be accused

Speak stone to be a stainless steel and fulfill your deepest will
to win the battle of your soul

Don't feed the smiling greedy beast; the easy way is not for long
the merchandise of deception will take it all

Details make the difference, but you must be trained to recognize them
to comprehend how precious they are

Signs of life, unchallenged light
Unfathomed traces
the mercenaries of your missions
Do the toughest judgment for your own actions
Don't let your own court without ethical construction

The hardest battle　　　　　　　　　　　　　　　*(Refrain)*
against any enemy
but between you and you
the longest distance
Unfathomed traces the aid
for your hopeless hope
The greatest view
an invitation for the top

Everyone owns a mountain to climb
The altitude is not important
the purpose is the same
360 degrees the widest spectrum
Self-esteem your best companion

The popular stability
is only for the dead
don't let it kill your breath
Everyone's life
is like an empty bottle
tough choices and efforts
filling it up drop by drop
the unfathomed traces add
the desirable flavor and aroma
the more full it is
the better person you are
It measures the longest distance
between you
and yourself

Challenge the bigger and the stronger
Deny the weight on your shoulder
Prescribe the unlimited border
No doubts should make you wonder

The hardest battle   *(Refrain)*
against any enemy
but between you and you
the longest distance
Unfathomed traces the aid
for your hopeless hope
The greatest view
an invitation for the top

Inception

Under the handmade lace, you searched your freedom
Always foreigners around you, they think they know you
Inside you a lion with unbalanced balances hungry from ambition
In the basement your first meeting with the seductive silence

You did what anybody can do to find the stairs for the ground floor
The recognition of the strangers soon moved you to the second floor
They don't think they love you, that's why they cannot bother you
Alone and loneliness are two divergent views, in a separate role

Money has no kin with success, is just the measurement of the poor
You are not a watermelon on a pair of scales; don't sell your time by the kilo
You imagine high glass towers in your mind, but never ever forget that the ropes of the marionettes are too close from their neck

This road is not your road
this sun is not your sun
Without freedom you can't decide
Nothing, but nothing is enough…

Defeat is the most precious *(Refrain)*
detail of inception
Quick success
the definition of deception
Lose the battles you can afford
on purpose

Don't let anyone take
your authenticity away
not to leave your fingerprints
without a name

There are no luxury cocoons, even in the highest floors or districts
Scrape the paper-thin walls with your signature, to open a hole
for the oxygen to enter; even butterflies fly away when it's time
It's impossible to abandon, only the trophies you don't deserve

The dirty nails from the soil, the lack of air in the mines
the stench of the garbage, the burned skin from the hot bitumen
or worse, the dirty hands from lawless laws behind a desk
can't gain your pride when you can't raise your look up to the sky

Difficult experiences are the sparks to fire up the real life
don't tolerate, but confront them to initiate your true inception
Otherwise you will be in limbo and maybe you will never wake up
your worst nightmare to be free than to depend on someone else

This hope is not your hope
this life is not your life
Without freedom you can't survive
Nothing, but nothing is enough…

Defeat is the most precious *(Refrain)*
detail of inception
Quick success
the definition of deception
Lose the battles you can afford
on purpose
Don't let anyone take
your authenticity away
not to leave your fingerprints
without a name

Generations
hand in hand
moved the heaviest stones
for their own inception
Don't waste not even one drop
from your tears and sweat
for the wrong direction
The illusions of conformism
make you compromise
with the worst infection

Is never too late
to unleash your deepest will, desires and beliefs
Is never too late
to dive in your own source of unlimited resources
Is never too late
to activate your real true inception
Is never too late
to deny your own deception
Is never too late
never too late

Discover and work hard
with your talents of any kind
which are your natural identity
Without them you will be blind
but you will think that you see
lost in the abyss of deception
When even fifteen minutes
of true real living are enough

This smile is not your smile
those eyes are not your eyes
Without freedom you can't be alive
Nothing, but nothing is enough…

Defeat is the most precious (Refrain)
detail of inception
Quick success
the definition of deception
Lose the battles you can afford
on purpose
Don't let anyone to take
your authenticity away
not to leave your fingerprints
without a name

No one sees with your eyes
No one laughs with your mouth
No one bleeds with your blood
No one will hold your hand just not to kneel
but to stand

Nothing, but nothing is enough…
Till you find the greatest motive
for your new real true life

Restless Victory

The horses neigh, the metals crackle
The courage screams battle cries
Their bodies are the canvas of war
Their compass lost in immortality
Every massacre didn't even consider happening again

Outnumbered or not, it doesn't matter at all
Excuses don't exist, only the reasons count
Do you have the vision of the greater good?
Or do you just follow a fool's orders, you never met?

Serve your weaker brothers
to give you the knowledge
Reborn from your worst defeat
and from your ashes win
Let cynicism hammer you like steel
unbreakable to be
Then the war will be petrified
the peace to be enforced

There is no victory without a battle *(Refrain 1)*
Don't just be happy in your claustrophobic morals
You are not alone in this immoral world
Seize the spoils of war for others to follow
and share them without sorrow

Don't let victory defeat you   *(Refrain 2)*
Plant the seeds of fear in the fields of wisdom
Dig in the plough share deep in the soil,
to protect the enemy from another mistake
Restless victory the highest glory

Merciless look, the teeth one mass
Determination is the only choice
the war of the worlds never ends
Arrogance of nothing against courtesy of inspiration
The smart history never gave the last trophy

Righteousness is the young cousin of justice
Knowledge is the unborn child of wisdom
If you are not related, retreat before the blade touches your skin
The endurance to suffer the decay is not capable of making you happy

Greed must be defeated inside its own field
to be taught
Ignorance must be victimized never to be used
as an excuse
Vanity must be vandalized
not to choose to be born again
The wolf will sleep near the sheep
only when the angry lion is watching

There is no victory without a battle   *(Refrain 1)*
Don't just be happy in your claustrophobic morals
You are not alone in this immoral world
Seize the spoils of war for others to follow
and share them without sorrow

Don't let victory defeat you   (Refrain 2)
Plant the seeds of fear in the fields of wisdom
Dig in the plough share deep in the soil,
to protect the enemy from another mistake
Restless victory the highest glory

From every crossroad
take the road without the fog
either way the sacrifices are unavoidable
you have to know
Easy privileges diminish
the visibility you own
Construct your spiritual missiles
than a covered face holding a stone
Thousands ask for their own rights from the few
is just a show

You endured
the minus decrees of the frost
You built your house
on the highest mountain
You discovered
numerous new lands
You invented
countless inventions

You are an Eskimo from Tibet,
an explorer, an inventor, a pioneer
You are humanity
Be restless
to win for us again
No one is neutral
till the very end

There is no victory without a battle   *(Refrain 1)*
Don't just be happy in your claustrophobic morals
You are not alone in this immoral world
Seize the spoils of war for others to follow
and share them without sorrow

Don't let victory defeat you   *(Refrain 2)*
Plant the seeds of fear in the fields of wisdom
Dig in the plough share deep in the soil,
to protect the enemy from another mistake
Restless victory the highest glory

Fallen Idol

The decay covered the land
the leaden sky seemed like a sun
the people expelled true values
to the caves sentenced for life

The bureaucratic temples respected as churches
the plastic puppets became leaders
moving pictures with oxy welding smiles
broadcasted very beautiful lies

Muted voices for the weak, the poor, the people's cry
The cavemen whisper to them to rise
not because the caves are not comfortable
but the truth shouldn't die

Behind the make-up of flaws   *(Refrain)*
the fallen idol exposed
taught to speak in front of a machine
Caveman, give us our dignity
Caveman, bring back the dreams we used to have
Caveman, save us
Nothing is ours, find your caves
not to hide, but to rise

The certificates defined anyone's future
Printed colored papers wanted to buy the sky
People were talking only about numbers
Inside the caves the only sparks of life

Ruthless selfishness renamed as solidarity
The rotten served in a modern package as fresh
Someone else's words became your personality
The roots of our true spirit in a small flower pots

Muted voices for prosperity, perspectives, for people's smiles
but the cavemen whisper to them to shine
not because the caves are not luxury
but humanity shouldn't die

Behind the make-up of flaws *(Refrain)*
the fallen idol exposed
taught to speak in front of a machine
Caveman, give us our dignity
Caveman, bring back the dreams we used to have
Caveman, save us
Nothing is ours, find your caves
not to hide, but to rise

You are like a drop against the ocean
You are like a used pen without ink
You must serve in order to lead
You are nothing more than a falling idol of sin

You think that you are a protagonist in a global scene
but you are a supernumerary in a local theater of absurdity
The cavemen know, but the people must see you fall
The fear of death has already imprisoned your life

You shouldn't even imagine becoming a legend
to see one
You shouldn't want to be a leader
to be one
You shouldn't dream of being a general
to act like one

You shouldn't care for glory
to earn it

Loud voices of admiration, don't let you feel that the time is
running out
but the cavemen whisper to you, there is no one else to blame
not because the caves are not warm
but your narcissism will not remain

Behind the make-up of flaws *(Refrain)*
the fallen idol exposed
taught to speak in front of a machine
Caveman, give us our dignity
Caveman, bring back the dreams we used to have
Caveman, save us
Nothing is ours, find your caves
not to hide, but to rise

But the time for criticism has come
because loans weren't available
to buy ignorance any more
The fallen idols thought they had power
and the war has just begun

The Cell of Kingdom

Our kingdom like a glass tower
high, low and the middle class
the boiling sparks on the basement
become the smoke of the cigars on top
but the lubricant cleaned easier than guilt
necessary loops like cows, to be accepted
useful only for a restaurant's reservation

Even then all want to go up than away
to sacrifice ears, tongues and eyes
for new toys, but only stitches remain
the communication is impossible
technology worse than wired paper cups
when egoism is the main nutrition
watches the sunglasses in the dark

Our world an arena of defeat
the gladiator who doesn't listen to the crowd, is banned for life
the losers can go up, ready to obey someone who has obeyed
but who is going to win in the end?

Our kingdom became a cell   *(Refrain)*
because we are not good enough
only to show, only to sell
Become
a tamer of horses
a tamer of lions
a tamer of the beast you used to be
In papyrus leaves

humanity
our only heritage

The few owners have the keys to watch
they are laughing, but they want to cry
outside the colorful gardens of salvation
the exit doors unlock, but almost untouched
because some wants to change the rules
not let the fire unify us, but our will
unfortunately masses need the plastic dreams

There is no religion of confusion
no national flag of discrimination
only artificial intelligence with skin
has the illusion of different interests
on the same trembling foundations
to wound us all and be wounded
to hunt us all and be hunted
to betray us all and be betrayed

Our world a merciful challenge
An extra bite or drop of water in one side, can kill a child in the other
We all pull the same rope, others with bleeding hands and others with manicures
but who is going to win in the end?

Our kingdom became a cell *(Refrain)*
because we are not good enough
only to show, only to sell
Become
a tamer of horses
a tamer of lions
a tamer of the beast you used to be
In papyrus leaves
humanity
our only heritage

We all born naked
the difference starts from a baby's bed
but only those for sale have bars

Insanity not to see it
Crime not to care about it
Riot to oppose it
Revolution not to adapt it
Evolution to change it

Our world a wheel of fortune
documents describe the possessions you think you own
when someone else controls even the supplies of your home

Our kingdom became a cell *(Refrain)*
because we are not good enough
only to show, only to sell
Become
a tamer of horses
a tamer of lions
a tamer of the beast you used to be
In papyrus leaves
humanity
our only heritage

The night quarrel not discussed in the elevator
The smiles of fake success cheat with cheeks
Sheep with bells hidden within paper bull's replicas
The birthday cake celebrates a day, not a lifetime
Why the parties of moments must be crowded anyway

Loyalty of Duty

A chained tiger is trying to be unleashed
the claws are scratching the wooden floor
the roars are looking the ray of light
from the almost closed door
It was just a dream

you wake up near the egocentric trust of fatal beauty
Do you even know the smell of love?

Thorns with honey are not only sweet
Substances don't have the best taste
The drums of awakening inside you
before the sirens from the outside world

Consciousness your main ally
Trust is a privilege inside the dust
Brave experience every responsibility
Ambitions mustn't be thirsty for long
Simple pleasures need to become desires
The moonlight will be there again
Memorable lifetime only before the end

Everything counted with numbers
except the few which are forgotten

Loyalty of duty among limited choices
right or wrong
Rope-walkers between everything and nothing
Some are stronger and others weaker than you

Kneel with pride only in front of the unreachable
Give a helping hand, to change the way of life
and the road will guide you

Armies against you   *(Refrain)*
An army with you
An oath of principles
your destination
Make time to wonder
make time to count
and when you are there
you will know

The broken wing forces you to walk
under the heavy sky, in a desert of mud
use your hands only the nose must be in air
Don't get tired till the end of the endless curve
It was just a dream

you wake up near documented guidelights of your destiny
Do you even imagine what it is?

Don't dream luxury coffins
cars, houses and five stars hotels
Needs are the shield of deception
Willingness the sword of fulfillment

Fortunes can buy only cement
to build a stepping stone higher
Materials and names are not heritage
We are all equal in God's eyes
we have just to make Him proud
The vastness of a possible invisible veil
altruism wins the games of purpose

We have no possessions
actions our only belongings

Loyalty of duty among limited choices
bad or good
Rope-walkers between history and gossips
Some are richer and others poorer than you
Don't pay homage to whatever shines
Treat the homeless like kings, to be treated like one
on this side or the other

Armies against you *(Refrain)*
An army with you
An oath of principles
your destination
Make time to wonder
make time to count
and when you are there
you will know

The uniqueness of our existence can't endure
with dictations of the past
or the fear of an unknown tomorrow
If you can't find your way
open a new one

Is not your duty
to serve a country, which didn't serve you
to honor a flag, which didn't honor you
to recognize a society, which didn't recognize you
to express traditions, which don't express you
to respect friendships, which didn't respect you
Loyalty of duty can't be used as an excuse

Armies against you   (Refrain)
An army with you
An oath of principles
your destination
Make time to wonder
make time to count
and when you are there
you will know

Was it just a dream?
Nobody can tell you till you know

Better die for a vision
than be without
Just to survive not to live
is not enough
to be a fugitive
from your own will
Be loyal to your only duty
the commitment of truthful life

I am No One

United the open palms full of seeds, emptied with courtesy to the beggar's hands
I am no one

The back on the bigger muted wave to protect the small child on the public beach
I am no one

The shout in the small backstreet to keep untouched and unharmed the young girl
I am no one

The glass of fresh water waged gentle to the mouth of the handicap grandfather
I am no one

Life is a ruthless *bras de fer* of hard and pure logic
That's why I want to be no one
No one at all
A trophy without recipient
A medal of honor without a name

But even if I am a root of grass
in a handful of sand
inside an empty ark
I will wait for the rain

In travail the craziness of logic   (Refrain)
I don't care about fame
I want the world to change
But
I will meet you without golden watch
I will treat you without a white robe
I will teach you without charges of lust
Because I am you

A dance with the lonely grandmother to make her remember how to smile
I am no one

The friendly thump on the back of the pupil who just failed in the exams
I am no one

The plan to make your dreams come true, to earn happiness no matter what
I am no one

The envelop at midnight under the door of grief before the foreclosure
I am no one

Life is a ruthless *bras de fer* of hard and pure reality
That's why I want to be no one
No one at all
A prize without address
Just an umbrella in the rain

But even if I am a worthless coin
in the middle of the ocean
inside an old shipwreck
I will wait for a rescue

In travail the craziness of logic (Refrain)
I don't care about fame
I want the world to change
But
I will meet you without golden watch
I will treat you without a white robe
I will teach you without charges of lust
Because I am you

Titles hunted with passion
to give recognition
when recognition should have been earned earlier
to make changes
when changes should have been already approved

Just for an iron spoon with golden paint
inside the saucepan of someone else's soup
but the rust will appear, sooner or later

Morning vans full of papers
are picturing the new victims
especially in the first pages
Trains loaded with rumors
describing ships without sailors

In travail the craziness of logic (Refrain)
I don't care about fame
I want the world to change
But
I will meet you without golden watch
I will treat you without a white robe
I will teach you without charges of lust
Because I am you

Solid

The progressive crusaders of hope
don't change the color of the sea
the blood must circulate in veins
but not in vain, with strong pulses
high and low for new beginnings

Emblems higher than us, to be seen
flags are waving with the same air
only colors are different, to identify us
without asking at least who we really are
in a vastness of the exact same emotions

What chain your hand not to shake it with another?
No one else to blame
Fair and unfair in your own country
Tears and smiles in your neighborhood
No foreign ruler is around

We march till we find each other *(Refrain)*
We drink the same bitterness
Same glass half full, half empty
Little sugar on the teaspoon for the few
And we march
on each other's shoulders
a new horizon to see
And we march and we march
till the end of our days
solid to be

The same problems, the same mistakes
The same pain from sins, the same rain
Different languages, but same meanings
An earlier sunrise with the same sun
a later moonlight with the same colors

The spirits are destroyed like old furniture
every day life is dying by holding our hands
ideologies desperately try to cover the gap
but our fundamental presence is absent
everything eaten from within, without us

What chains your feet with an iron ball?
It's only your fault
Love and hate inside your own society
Stronger and weaker in your team
No foreign enemy is around

We march till we find each other *(Refrain)*
We drink the same bitterness
Same glass half full, half empty
Little sugar on the teaspoon for the few
And we march
on each other's shoulders
a new horizon to see
And we march and we march
till the end of our days
solid to be

The imperialism of spirit a prelude of democracy
any heavy truce can't enforce ceasefire for long
a persuasive foreign breast won't feed you eternally
and war will be the only messenger of true truth
the baby's bib of enjoyment will be exchanged

Every day a stamp with a new sealing wax
Today shouldn't remember yesterday
This year shouldn't remember the previous
The decade shouldn't remember anything
Solid to be as a whole, some day tomorrow

An entire new world inside you
surrendered from a future marriage
makes you an invisible naked acrobat
in the unwritten dogma of sacrifices
A gentle dilemma inside a raw abyss
tangible or unreachable
mediocrity or uniqueness
bureaucracy or actions
material or spiritual
recognition or success
education or wisdom
protection or freedom
price or priceless
tradition or civilization
national or global

table without a chair
or chair without a table?

No deadlock chains our necks
we march the exit to find
solid to be as spirit, heart and soul, one body
to be reborn as beings and then as a whole
any foreign invader, is just the excuse

We march till we find each other   *(Refrain)*
We drink the same bitterness
Same glass half full, half empty
Little sugar on the teaspoon for the few
And we march

on each other's shoulders
a new horizon to see
And we march and we march
till the end of our days
solid to be

and we march
and we march
and we march
solid to be

Fugitives of Trust

The palaces are always clean
because the bribery named job
Masses with shavings of silence
are just a nightmare in the sleep

The knowledge slips from father to son
From the hammered iron till a milestone
legacies for the neighbor you never met
not for a goal, but for the hope for hope

but whom to trust
charities arm in arm with ambitions
mosses and lichens for a lobster

It is not trust
to let the baker keep your bread
but to the hungry when you starve
is not only to keep a secret sealed
but to change the reasons of its source

Dynasties of dust   *(Refrain)*
behind the portraits of ancestors
anonymity born the legacies
bravery the legends
but whom to trust
when you see the swamp like a green grass
the limits of the sky as new perspectives

Which leaf to trust in spring?
Better wait for the autumn
To count the odds of decency
is like a thunder in the snow

Trust is worth it when not mentioned
Songs jealous the depth of the words
poems envy the popularity of refrains
music can gather all in a magic sound

but whom to trust
compassion in a very small bottle
drunk with expensive champagnes

It is not trust
to cry for help and to be rescued
but not to be in danger
precious but earned when unnecessary
otherwise must be offered

Dynasties of dust *(Refrain)*
behind the portraits of ancestors
anonymity born the legacies
bravery the legends
but whom to trust
when you see the swamp like a green grass
the limits of the sky as new perspectives

Trust is the rags of a great cause, fugitive in a foreign yard
Where are the lumbermen of the trees of suspicions?
Where are the bullfighters of the bull of compromises?
Where are the maps for the destination of happiness?
All become the taxi drivers to transport endless hopes

Whom to trust
when you tell lies you don't believe
when you stay small you can't feel the big
when you are arrogant you can't see defeat

Whom to trust
in a world with shine shoes and naked feet
we all are fugitives without shield
when the neighbor is on fire you will be burned from it

Whom to trust
nobody will believe you for a greater cause
popular the knitting of the sweaters of egoism
butter and marmalade for any enemy
makes us vulnerable for ever

Dynasties of dust *(Refrain)*
behind the portraits of ancestors
anonymity born the legacies
bravery the legends
but whom to trust
when you see the swamp like a green grass
the limits of the sky as new perspectives

PART C

Synchronized Steps

Chapter Five
Character: inference

Tracing pace: search

Borderless Eyes

A tear falls when the wings just lift up only dust
but the barren earth needs even this tiny drop
as you need to be trained hard, to get stronger
to be prepared, because to fly needs duration

Every day is a great teacher with precious details
to make you learn to add the past in the senses
but if you gag any today, your ears will become deaf
only to see what you want, not what's existing

There is one promise
you have to fulfill
the one to yourself

Keep your sight *(Refrain)*
to the wide-open sky
to become borderless
success
doesn't fill up the eyes
but the heart
the victory

to be the fulfillment of the soul
the glory
to be unnecessary

The perfect watch doesn't show the moments
its functionality offers the accuracy of efficiency
to put what you have to do in a sack of amnesia
not to count just to be there, but to be on time

The only sensor that time has, leads to the timing
to learn through running to be quicker by walking
but if you gag the seconds, the hours will become blind
only to be where you must, not where you please

There is one court
you have to answer
the one inside you

Keep your sight *(Refrain)*
to the wide-open sky
to become borderless
success
doesn't fill up the eyes
but the heart
the victory
to be the fulfillment of the soul
the glory
to be unnecessary

The defeat is helping you
to realize the right course
to understand
if it is what you want
if it is what you wish
if it is what you dream
if it is what you need

because nothing is happening at once
needs to observe you, to tease you, to trouble you, to streak you
to change your limited limits
to show you
that you can go a hundred times further
as when a metallic bar is few meters from the floor
you can hold it for some seconds or minutes
but when under your feet is a huge gap
you will grab it for hours
at the exact very moment
your strong will for life prevails
that's why any achievement due to the same cause
needs to be persuaded
that you will never abandon
to deserve it by overcoming yourself
but if you want the highest glory
which has nothing to do with fame
you must be unbreakable

The visible
is beyond what you can see
the tangible
is beyond what you can touch
the sensible
is beyond what you can feel
because life
is beyond what you can imagine

Your intelligence must be hammered
to become sharper
but don't bother it
to calculate numbers
when a machine can do it better
to know all the flags
when they are in the internet
to remember presidents

when you never met them
to memorize history
when you have to build the future

Search in an ocean
to find knowledge
not identity
to fall in love with new thoughts
to become ideas
from simple letters
to create humble words
gathered in your speech
to revitalize new meanings
your actions to promote
higher perspectives

The alternative
doesn't choose particular names
the fantasy
to have no borders
the tears
to have no barriers
the happiness
to have no boundaries
the wishes
to have no barricades
because
freedom can't be given
must be earned

Keep your sight   *(Refrain)*
to the wide-open sky
to become borderless
success doesn't fill up the eyes
but the heart
the victory
to be the fulfillment of the soul
the glory to be unnecessary

I will never give limits to my expectations
even if I have no place to stay
because I have to fulfill my self-realization

I will never give limits to my thoughts
even if I have the most smart devices
because I choose when to push the buttons

I will never give limits to my vision
even if I have the biggest fortune
because I am search for the essences

I will never give limits to my feelings
even if the smell of your skin resurrects my breath
not to belittle you
because I am still alive

Dogma of Menace

Where is the difference when a cartoon informs the news
than a paid criminal which is ready to say anything for money
public loud-hailers can urge people to run against the walls
by reassuring them sufficiently that it's for their own safety

Nice articles can encourage parents to throw their kids from a cliff
relaxing with pictures of trampolines which will make them happy
all to wait for the talent of the loudest voice, to warn for the truth
which no one will ever know, because the rulers write the history

If in the burnt books
was written the righteousness
why peace didn't prevail

Unwritten the undeclared *(Refrain)*
dogma of menace
retaliates with anything
just to do something
juvenile behavior
in adults' bodies
Spare me
I did no wrong
Spare those
who brought the change
at your door

The people becomes slot-machines to be able to function
is not different if they need coins or millions of banknotes
the diminished will transform them gradually into machines
asking for rights when it is easier to be replaced from robots

We are born with artificial intelligence, from zero to grow
engines with same capacity can combine only the existing
only our God-given inspirations can create the brand-new
mechanisms just give us surplus of time to be more human

If only few are responsible
and all the rest innocent
why we don't live as we desire

Unwritten the undeclared *(Refrain)*
dogma of menace
retaliates with anything
just to do something
juvenile behavior
in adults' bodies
Spare me
I did no wrong
Spare those
who brought the change
at your door

The arrogance is been initiated
from the illusion of possessions
when we are here only to serve
we cannot dominate
in Someone Else's Kingdom
and the more being given
the bigger is the responsibility
to share

The confusion of misused abilities
enters inside the recipe
which transform humans into machines
through compromises
and starts for just one day
but what is a month
extended in some years
which can become decades
one day with a duration of three months
can become a lifetime

In maximum three years
any ordinary business can run properly
any task will build foundations
any job will find its limits
and then the carrier must search for new potential
because we spend the majority of our lives at work
that's why it must be extraordinary
not to be a destructive habit
like an unproductive decoration of the same goods
to try through consumption to cover an increased gap
which will be wider every single day

Depended interests are called to vote
ready to choose the easy for the ears
which also can be paid to betray
in statistics known for a year before
the same from noon till afternoon
in elections of virtual needs not perspectives
to elect fewer than the fingers of a palm
which no one knew before
without any achievement
but just the capacity to maintain a habit
in polarized environments
with subjects which should have never appeared
to gain parliamentary majorities

like the rest deputies want to harm their own country
when all of them represent the exact same system
which is just asking where to consume its artificial energy
and when it brings the crisis
if it can afford it
is faking changes
by using the same people
with different faces

The machines cannot love,
cannot feel, cannot believe
just have missions without visions
and if you diminish your senses
you will become one
capable to be only a gear of a system
which has no reason to have feelings any more
unable to succeed among so many identical replacement parts
because when the role of its citizens neutralizes
the meaning of any state is confused
lost in a procedural invisible decision
who should serve who

Machines can replace only machines
not humans
but the incapacity to develop
emotional intelligence
and to progress also your authenticity
makes you function like a mechanism
able only to be evaluated from a particular efficiency
to fill up yourself inside boxes with predicted results
and our necessary evolution
to be exposed in front of the eyes
of wars and women

From homo erectus
to homo sapiens
and now to homo futuris
which is our choice
for our future

Unwritten the undeclared　　　　　　　　　　　　　　*(Refrain)*
dogma of menace
retaliates with anything
just to do something
juvenile behavior
in adults' bodies
Spare me
I did no wrong
Spare those
who brought the change
at your door

Our organism is a perfect engine
but we must make efforts to become persons
the uniqueness each one of us has
to count

As the population increases
it will be far more difficult
to find an identity in a catalogue
and the laws will help us
not to live like animals
but when more and more
choose to work just for the fuel
the unfair will rise
because we need resources
till the end of the day

The inspirations will be always available
to create brand-new productive pillars
the sources to provide the infinity
with clear capacity to bring justice
to make us able to live like humans
as so many claims
that we are

Fundamental pace: can

Nuances of Existence

We didn't create the seeds
but even those small entities want to grow
need to be cultivated and watered to become bigger
after a difficult period to be capable to offer

Ask the middle class
when they don't accept any change to occur
should they ask for more or for less?

Ask the homeless
why they are sleeping on the benches
from their own failures or from ours?

Ask the thieves
why they want to steal the wealthy places
for survival or for pleasure?

Ask the nurses
why they are awake all night to treat the sick
to pay their bills or to offer?

Ask the students
why they have to study so many heavy books
to gain grades or knowledge?

Put yourself in
others' positions
be them for a while
to be selfless
to search for reasons
because what is easy for you
can be difficult for someone else
and the opposite

Different universes
in the same world
which one do you choose?

Row   *(Refrain 1)*
you, lazy selfishness
Row
to reach the coast
Row
the waves of the ocean
will drown us all
Row

What happens   *(Refrain 2)*
with good will
offers
otherwise
destroys

We didn't paint the color of our skin
everything that nature gives us must be respected
but we can criticize the actions and the consequences
without extolling what shines and condemning what doesn't

Ask the racists
when they have to follow someone else to survive
should they search for reasons or for enemies?

Ask the gun owners
why they have already accepted their premature death
to protect lives or things?

Ask the corrupt
why they trespass on others' preserves to keep their luxuries
for a need or for desire?

Ask the bodyguards
why they protect even dictators or the worst rich criminals
for money or for ideology?

Ask the wage-earners
why they support any system just to gain their bread
they give enough effort or they are afraid to live?

Put yourself out
of your own situations
and watch them as a third party
like a cold-blooded spectator
to be objective
to search for transparence
because what seems legal
can be a major crime

Different egos
in the same body
which one do you use?

Row   *(Refrain 1)*
you, lazy selfishness
Row
to reach the coast
Row
the waves of the ocean
will drown us all
Row

The innocence must sweat (Refrain 3)
to bring justice
because
the guilt must cry
to find salvation

Imagine if all
the citizens would upgrade their role of this ultimate title
to stop any wrongdoing
the innovators will follow their visions with faith
no matter what
the entrepreneurs will invest continuously to the new
to care only to create more perspectives
the artists will express fanatically their own identity
without any compromise
the employees will find what they can do best
to be the new prospects
the bosses will put everyone in the right position
without banning the better ideas of their own
the part-timers will be focused on what they want
not to lose their destination for a salary
the manual workers will make one more dream with
each callus
to be always independent
the doctors will expect their fees from the cures
not from heavy wallets
the lawyers will subject in close scrutiny all the laws
not to let anyone to be unfair
the civil servants will be obliged to serve the people
not their virtual recruiters
the governors will have a vision for a brighter future
without thinking of themselves
then debts will not be created any longer
and loyalty will be for free
because titles don't make
the roles or the professions

but the produced qualities
explain their necessity

We all are on the same ocean liner
where the fair holds the helm
the more we support the wrong
leads us into the middle of the ocean
and even if the weather is good
the unsatisfied on its lower levels
will attempt to open a hole in the keel
because they already living their own wreck
so what difference does it make
to happen for all the rest?
but even if we do the right thing
by understanding our real needs
and we change our minds at the last moment
the reefs will make their presence

If you put water in your wine
just everything to be easier
cheated from bigger life expectance
you have to consider
what kind of living has
no flavors, no colors, no tastes?
have no senses the securities without breath
but they are hiding in cocoons
which becoming prisons
never to let even a butterfly
be free

What faith
doesn't want to genuflect?
what love
doesn't want to hug?
what hope
doesn't want efforts?

what wish
doesn't want a destination?
what purpose
doesn't want a reason?
what life
doesn't want a meaning?
the tears
to bring redemption

By accepting the unacceptable
you will lose your powers
and when you find some weaker
you will exert pressure to punish them
for your own failures
to imagine that you are strong
automatic reactions will change your sense of reality
to protect yourself from the truth
to be proud in front of your family
for one more day
to appear as a leader
for one more day
to feel successful
for one more day
to keep your privileges
for one more day
to think that you are alive
for one more day
but the canker will consecutively gnaw the tomorrows
together with everything you believe you own
and no matter how many years it lasts
the virtual glory will always be
just for one more day

Who is right   (Refrain 4)
and who is wrong
we all are able to know
if we care to find
the architecture of truth
but who wants to adapt it
in a world who runs
without running

It's not a problem the incompetent rulers
who are tough only with others not with themselves
and they care only for their personal interests not the people
but their followers
who are the reason for the establishment
of totalitarian regimes
or derailed disguised democracies
by executing even cruel orders without thinking
and using unreal lame excuses to do it
like to feed their families
when they will never give to their assignors
to keep their children
not even for an hour

If you feel that it is a necessity
to be a racist
be for the right reasons
which is not the color of the skin
or small minorities
which are already vulnerable
and definitely not the people with disabilities
who are the real fighters by nature
icons for the rest of us
capable only to upgrade their families and cynical societies
but with those who continuously
are doing the wrong things on purpose
like the criminals who make others to suffer
for their own pleasure

You need courage to avoid majorities
which are following the wrong
but you can separate yourself from bad attitudes
like stupidity
which doesn't concern those with low IQ
is always enough to make them happy
but the smart who think that they are smarter
like the power without foundations
like the arrogance of nothing
like the undeserved wealth
like the lazy poverty
which without doing anything
blames others for everything
and even if you want
to give them more chances
for their compliance
you will never support them
but radicalization can be only useful
when it is predetermined
one inglorious end

In our world
no one cares for excuses
but facts

Humanitarianism
has no geographical preferences
on the maps are shaped the border lines
which usually are not visible on the landscapes

Row *(Refrain 1)*
you, lazy selfishness
Row
to reach the coast
Row
the waves of the ocean

will drown us all
Row

The innocence must sweat　　　　　　　　　　　　(Refrain 3)
to bring justice
because
the guilt must cry
to find salvation

Dig into your thoughts
dig into your ideas
dig into your inspirations
dig into your feelings
dig into your intuitions
dig into your reasons
dig into your senses
to create your own foundations
to stabilize your security walls
no sledgehammer to be able
not even to crack them

If you bend your head
to earn the livelihood
one day you will lose it
and you will protest among others
who made the same mistake
but if you do it for a bigger fortune
one day you will be lucky to have the chance
to explain the unexplainable to a court

The only honest way
is to believe in yourself
without doubts
to invest your time on your tendencies
which are your competitive advantages
to lead you to develop your real talents

and the pocket will always have enough
to accommodate you with sufficiency
to be where you always wanted
by discovering
your very own nuance of existence

Penetrative pace: want

Uncharted Waters

Be afraid of the permanent which will become a predicted habit
is nothing else there than raw materials in strangers' ball of fibers
the time must weave the carpet with a variety of solved enigmas
to create the abilities one day to fly where you dared to imagine
because the real stability is the result of an unstoppable evolution

Who said
that passion
doesn't include logic?

Who said
that inspirations
are not your destination?

Who said
that ideas
are not your missions?

Who said
that victory
doesn't have a cost?

Who said
that without a vision
you can be alive?

What you are now
was uncharted waters
some years ago

What appears as a risk *(Refrain 1)*
it isn't
what seems as the main avenue
takes longer to see the contrary
because we have to fall
to comprehend our weight
as the only way
to create a true beginning

Be afraid of the ports you already walked, have nothing more to give
just offer a motive to generate thoughts from existing infrastructures
to find unused or new ones without manuals with described promises
to construct alternative angles or to discourage from them the spiders
because the true sustainability is the outcome of an incessant progress

Who said
that certificates
make the scientists?

Who said
that prizes
make the heroes?

Who said
that papers
can describe people?

Who said
that wisdom
can be studied?

Who said
that without your authenticity
you are still alive?

What is obvious today
was uncharted waters
some decades ago

Kill first   *(Refrain 2)*
what ends last
the hope
to embrace the uncharted waters
and when the difficult times
unavoidably will come
not to abandon
not to surrender
not to die as a hero
but to live like one

It's not a business to recycle existing needs
what difference does it make
if the electricity bill
comes from the private or the public sector?
the light has already the highest speed
and the management in any case
must search for skills not political reliance

The real entrepreneurship
must be occupied with the new
to speak loud without words
by preaching the future not the past
to tease the curiosity
and to make the market run without sweating
through new creative ideas to be expanded a healthy growth
their enhanced width to lead also the financial markets
by holding them tight hand in hand
both to surge with productive liquidity the real economy
and even if the pie can feed all the mouths worldwide
it needs different flavors
to be reliably viable without volatility

The manipulation can take place
only inside the flaws of a system
it cannot harm the innovative processes

or the progressive investments
but when they are absent
the glass starts to fill up to the brim
from the increasing debt
which indicates the mistakes of a failure
and when behaviors don't change
the time will make it more expensive
the countdown to be initiated
for the voluntary to be obligatory
everybody to start searching the creative producers of tomorrow
when their merciless eyes have ostracized them in the shadows
but what was costing one, by asking for mercy
it will become more than a thousand
given only if the world deserve it

Even the laws
want to be uncharted waters
by losing themselves through articles
between the past and the future
to enforce the universal law
because who doesn't know
what is right
but how many can afford it

Even the richest people have wishes
but they must be transparent to meet them
Every cleaning lady has dreams
but they must make efforts to fulfill them
All the public drivers know to read a map
but they must risk to find different destinations
The majority of the scientists want to make a step forward
but they shouldn't care for the sponsorships
Great amounts of engineers are capable of creating the new
but they shouldn't be influenced by the trends
Many professors consider creating the ideal citizens
but the results are after the period of the studies

A lot of unemployed have good ideas
but they must insist on fighting to realize them
Everyone who has been abandoned wants a better life
but the obstacles are necessary to understand the perfection
Those who live in the ordinary often are thinking of more
but they have to invest in the unusual which is around them
The advantages of some
as ideas or as funds
are the opportunities for others
in a coalition of true societies
seen as the only crucial message from the political parties
because justice is been derived from our actions
We all have to be determined
to exchange
the temporariness of the permanence
with the real living

Mediocrity is not life *(Refrain 3)*
but death with fake heart
Learn to swim on the uncharted waters
because no road
is strewed with rose-leaves
to become priceless
even if a price exists
to seize everything
by being prepared
to gain nothing

If you forgot what you always wanted
It is like you are dying without noticing it
because the silence of the majorities
don't consider
the suicide of the will as murder
that's why it has no verdict in the short-term
but in the long-term the punishment is unavoidable
by starting to harm the psychology

and as all the problems
must be identified first
in order to be solved
not to be approached
the point of no return

When you buy maps from ordinary stores
you will never find the location with the treasure
and your pension will be lower than what you expect
because the majorities find a bad idea
to mapmaking their own way
but in our world
the distance has a meaning
you have to discover the cactus
to search inside the bushes
your quest to show you
the tree with the peculiar shape
because everything is based on logic
and to understand the fruit
you must find its root

When no one cares to create the new
in any fashion
we will all live in a jungle
where the hyenas will dominate
and we will need more corpses
to feed them
the starving rubbish bins
will swallow also the useful
to change their taste from time to time
and the real heroes
who are the only ones
capable of preventing the worst
will vanish
the war to happen
never from one man's fault

everyone to become a hero
dead or alive
those who treat
and those who stole
those who fought and
those who hid on the branches
but none of them have won

The athletes try hard
to extend with traces
little by little
the necessity of a new more
from what we already know
by running a bit faster
by jumping a bit further
by throwing a bit longer
by swimming a bit stronger
by lifting a bit heavier
by enduring a bit better
by aiming a bit closer
and the clear colors of the flags
at the starting point
melts at the finish line
under a world record
as an achievement for all
reminding somehow the summits of the few
capable to gather all the nations together
by making them to protest often with clashes
against their own wider international friendship
which altogether has already established to be heard
called globalization

Kill first   (Refrain 2)
what ends last
the hope
to embrace the uncharted waters
and when the difficult times
unavoidably will come
not to abandon
not to surrender
not to die as a hero
but to live like one

Death is uncharted waters
is something that life can't imagine
and some who have an opinion about it
is difficult for others to believe them
because they are still alive
but we can be proud of our every day
to have better chances for the positive
never to be late

We don't know the future
but when you are afraid
of any unknown tomorrow
you are destroying
consciously or subconsciously
the dynamic potentials
of your any today

Who said
that the spotlights
make the protagonists?

Who said
that compromise
is life?

Who said
that people
are not important?

Who said
that leaders
have ambitions?

Rising pace: desire

Rhythm of Devotion

In an isolated derailed cell far from the glamorous civilization
are loudly clanging the chains of mankind's common sense
and when majorities get used to this noise, yells take its place
the necessary to be understood by stretching everyone's skin

Under the same shiny sky cooperate the cheaters and cheated
to convict the innocence by keeping the guilt without accusation
but the push trembles the iron door, unable to resist much longer
you must change your mind before the double locks are broken

One step
away
one step
more

The heart beats *(Refrain 1)*
when freedom lives
the triumph breathes
when from the darkness
even a speck
is searching
for the light
to find its rhythm of devotion

Be obliged not to have what you deserve
no tamer to be able to subdue your wild soul
your will to seize what you always wanted
to be in the position to desire without musts

Be a conqueror never to feel that you own a thing
by knowing that everything is been given as a gift
to become greater than you possibly can imagine
to have by far more to share for a better world

One breath
away
one breath
more

Faith of stainless steel *(Refrain 2)*
I am ready to meet my end
for what I believe
an army to confront me
must be ready to die
and if they conquer me
I will respect them
forever

Efficiency is not
what the people accept
but what the heart doesn't reject
to reduce the time through preparation
by working for what you always wanted to do
without thinking at all
if it's a popular profession or non-existing
and if you have no chances
fight harder to engage your desires
not to accept not even the smallest mistake
to experience your own victory
to be silent in a protest of a common will

not just to win
but to be saved

Don't put yourself in matrices
but create your very own
as we all are composed to be
and who will notice
if the lines under the eyes
of a wooden deer
are not perfect
when you can make it run

Do the best you can
without considering
what the others do
the actions of honor
construct your own infrastructures
canyons, rivers and seas
the pain to find a way out
till you will build
your own protection shield
hammered from a thousand problems
trained from them to be unbreakable

Believe the others
to be believed
trust, to be trusted
help, to be helped
protect, to be protected
respect, to be respected
love, to be loved
and when the unusual appears
the network will be ready
to confront it

The power of innocence
has unfinished ammunition
because it needs great courage
to be preserved
but you must go away from what you love the most
if you are not ready to give everything you got
you must deny the easy
to be able to endure the pain
the difficult to harm no more
thankful to bend in front of the weak
to make them stronger
unswerving to stand in front of the strong
to make them weaker
new balances to be found
new thoughts to be allowed
a new era to be possible
a new smile for the impossible

You need no contracts with yourself
an internal oath is enough
needs no guarantees the self-esteem
to overcome the unbelievable
by exchange what seems with the first look
as permanent, official or recognized
with a rusted key
which needs to be refined
to mobilize you
to search for the real treasury
no elsewhere but inside you
and contains just one map
to show you the only pathway
which leads to happiness

Be restless(Refrain 3)
without freedom
feel breathless
without a vision
to go against
the odds of today
to find the reasons
of tomorrow

Make the complicated
simple and meaningful
who cares to search in an ocean of words
for maybes
Be competitively sophisticated to
give to the raw a shape
give to a thought a body
give to a whisper a sound
give to the humble a pride
to make the unknown
known
what has no voice
to be heard
what is for good
to conquer
to be in the position to teach
what you never been taught

The money doesn't make the professionals
but the added value
is not important
to get paid to do something
but fundamental
with your specialized work to get what you require
without asking
as an unchallenged reward not as a tip
a productive market to be created

where the employees will provide the obvious
and the employers the unique
otherwise altogether
we will face a recession
without any exception

We are all born with spiritual myopia
to construct our own pair of spectacles
spectrum by spectrum
added from the experiences of knowledge
our visibility to be increased
but if you stick with the theory
it will offer sunglasses in the dark
to be blindfolded for what matters
and heavily diligent for what doesn't
unable to understand the better sight
because you will never know
what it's like to see
the perfect view

When it is very difficult
to give homelessness a shelter
because it gets used to its situation
just needs a blanket in the cold
imagine how more abrasive it is
to persuade the mediocrity
to get better
when it's lodged under overvalued roofs
and feels satisfied
just to be next in the line
with total ignorance how to invest in the future
because the easy makes it able only to consume
when someone else allows
by making it a subject with empty talks
but it's just a victim in a chess game
from where it's always absent
when every move must force a predicted reaction

If you swim in a swamp
because you think it's profitable
you are getting an undeserved wealth
always vulnerable
even to the most minor external vibrations
but creates the narcissism of possessions
to shine in front of the mirror
not to let you to notice
that you can't see
deep in your eyes

Don't pity
the alone boatman
who rows to meet the sunset
but those
who can't celebrate
without company
and they are trying to hide
in crowded isolations

You shouldn't be afraid of the different
because different you are
when it's maybe
the only thing
capable of saving you
unless if hordes of people
fight for a greater cause
unavoidable it will be enforced
but you shouldn't forget
that wars exist without weapons
never without victims

The attack (Refrain 4)
in the consciousness
never comes
from the good
and you have
to fight back
not to undermine
your heart

We have lived the dramas of destruction
caused from our own failures
but from the ashes
we have rebuilt our civilization
with a vision
in a promise
never to go back again
generations hand in hand
tried hard to bring us where we are
and from time to time
we have just to turn our heads
for only some moments
simply to tell them
that we made it

There is no age
unable to restart
there is no will
incapable to act
there is no life
incompetent to desire
there is no vengeances
unwilling to forget
there is no sin
careless to be redeemed

We all have a fire inside us
only for a noble cause
destined to become unquenchable
but it depends on you
if it will continue burning
or by diminishing it will perish
to transform the candlelight into conflagration
you shouldn't imagine, but act
you shouldn't dream, but visualize
you shouldn't abandon, but prioritize
you shouldn't try, but do
because the only one able to stop you
is you

Life is not about
getting something
neither far more than that
nor far less
but everything
Little by little
a little bit today
and the next day
and the next day
and the next day
the weight to be lighter
the destination to be closer
the dream to be a vision
true living to be a mission

I am getting closer
and closer
because
I overcame myself a hundred times
to learn that what seems as an end
just declares a new beginning
I have worked harder that I could imagined

I have reached levels without knowing that they exist
I have suffered more that I can endure
I have acknowledged my defeat
because I cannot do any of this one more time
but even if I have fallen
without knowing if I will stand again
I never stop believing
that's why
I am getting closer
and closer

I am coming closer
you are coming closer
we are coming closer
closer and closer
by increasing the magnitude
of your rhythm of devotion
all to be tuned
for the greater good

Rise *(Refrain 5)*
only the maximum
is life
there is no other
compensation
than a harmless truth
Rise

There is no country
to stop you
there are no horses
to take you back
there are no obstacles
to dissuade you
there is no determination
to let you be enslaved

The profound width of wisdom
makes us kneel from real admiration
in front of the courtesy of its magnificence
without dependences or orders
any other submission is just nickels

Grab your invisible chains
to eradicate them from the reasons
to come closer
and closer

Bite with your teeth the noose you put
to cut it off from your neck
to come closer
and closer

Throw the prefabricated profane excuses
for once and for all to the garbage
to come closer
and close

Punish your weaknesses
to become stronger
to come closer
and closer

Forget the needs of dependence
nothing to keep you down
to come closer
and closer

Aim for the highest targets
by pushing the door of your prison
to see that it's open

Don't be lost
in the alchemies of confusion
you cannot lie to the truth
Rise
from what you are

One purpose,
one life

COMPULSORY COMPENDIUMS

Collateral Pattern in the levels of always

We are all born without any birthright
nobody is an exception
the legacies can't be automatically inherited
because we have to seize our deepest will
the unconditional actions cultivate the spirit
intact our faith and values to inspire the ages
of a world lacking coincidences

Sincerely yours,
Victor Leonard Libermann

Marginal Note & Sample

This specialized clarification partially and briefly unveils the unfamiliar familiarity of the book's structural amenity, as a response to diligently supervise the numerical indication of the back cover. Its intellectual coherence is surgically analyzed in complete extent during the first pages, precociously to mobilize an undoubted further exploration.

Innovative Structure
Philosophy easy to read, expressed through extracts of subjects, innovatively structured as lyrics, to be more accessible and comprehensible; in order to offer its companionship to the smallest till the biggest idea, never to feel alone.

Further Inducements
The book contains 59 Subjects with 74 conflated Refrains, to inspire also the creation of new qualitative songs, composed with different words or parts of the existing ones; in order to speak with actions and its sight to spread with a wider width.

'My boat has a name and a soul
no one can take it from me
My heritage
a broken piece of wood
wet from a thousand seas'

Contents

THE MASTER BOOK
Introductory 7
Introduction 9
Simplified Short Biography 10
Foundations 11
Sample: part of 'Faith of Attraction' 11
The Compass 12

HUMANS AGAINST MACHINES (Inclusive)
Intellectual Coherence 15
Characteristics & Morphology 17
Samples of structural components 19
Samples of confirmation 22
Mentality & Biometrics 23

PART A
The prisoners with open doors
(Surrounding Title) 29
Chapter One
Character: comprehension 31
The Decay of Hope 31
Alarm Clock 35
The First from the End 38
Calculus 41
Biased Days 44
Unsung Hero 47
Unknown Nature 50
The Journey 53
Restricted Districts 56

Voice in the Crowd 59
The Stairs 62
Unswerving 67
Equilibrium 71
Chapter Two
Character: intensive 75
Seldom 75
Invisible Chain 78
Paper-skin 81
Roots 84
Parameters of Adjustment 88
The Vision Beyond 92
Fatal Acceptance 96
Ignition 99
The Autopsy of Rejection 103
Ground Zero 107
Without Verdict 111
The Mirror of Yesterdays 115
Unavoidable Passion 118
The Waves of Circumstances 123

IN OUR WORLD
Chapter Three
Character: extensive 129
The Fusion of Reaction 129
The Standing Man 133
The Deadline 138
The Unexpected 142
The Preconditions 146
Capital 150
Faith of Attraction 155
Useful Fear 159
Unseen Mercenaries 163
Premature 167
The Idiosyncrasy of Whys 171
The Amortization of a Dream 175

Reciprocal 179
The Width of Impact 184

PART B
Divided Heroes
(Central Title) 191
Chapter Four
Character: preliminary 193
Divided Heroes 193
Unchain Impossible 197
Screams of Silence 201
Invisible Absence 206
Unfathomed Traces 209
Inception 213
Restless Victory 217
Fallen Idol 221
The Cell of Kingdom 224
Loyalty of Duty 227
I am No One 231
Solid 234
Fugitives of Trust 238

PART C
Synchronized Steps 241
Chapter Five
Character: inference 243
Tracing pace: search 243
Borderless Eyes 243
Dogma of Menace 248
Fundamental pace: can 254
Nuances of Existence 254
Penetrative pace: want 264
Uncharted Waters 264
Rising pace: desire 273
Rhythm of Devotion 273

COMPULSORY COMPENDIUMS
Collateral Pattern
in the levels of always 287
Marginal Note & Sample 288

Rate this book on our website!

www.novum-publishing.co.uk

The author

Born in Thessaloniki in 1974, Victor Leonard Libermann had tough beginnings but trusted in his dreams and worked incredibly hard to fulfill them. He believes that sleeping and waking with the same vision until it becomes reality will wipe away the past. He currently builds financial systems for the confrontation of the Euro zone's debt crisis and the viability of the euro. The last ten years he is living across Europe to complete his mission.

novum PUBLISHER FOR NEW AUTHORS

The publisher

He who stops getting better stops being good.

This is the motto of novum publishing, and our focus is on finding new manuscripts, publishing them and offering long-term support to the authors.
Our publishing house was founded in 1997, and since then it has become THE expert for new authors and has won numerous awards.

Our editorial team will peruse each manuscript within a few weeks free of charge and without obligation.

You will find more information about
novum publishing and our books on the internet:

www.novum-publishing.co.uk